QUEEN OF
HEARTS

BY Jill Briscoe

How to Follow the Shepherd When You're Being Pushed Around by the Sheep (Formerly *How to Fail Successfully*)

Queen of Hearts

QUEEN OF HEARTS

The Role of Today's Woman

based on Proverbs 31

Jill Briscoe

Fleming H. Revell Company
Old Tappan, New Jersey

Unless otherwise identified, all Scripture quotations in this volume are from the King James Version of the Bible.

Scripture quotations identified MOFFATT are from THE BIBLE: A NEW TRANSLATION by James Moffatt. Copyright 1926 by Harper & Row, Publisher, Inc.; renewed 1954 by James A.R. Moffatt. Reprinted by permission of the publisher.

Verses marked TLB are taken from The Living Bible, copyright © 1971 by Tyndale House Publishers, Wheaton, IL. Used by permission.

Scripture quotation identified RSV is from the Revised Standard Version of the Bible, copyrighted 1946, 1952 © 1971 and 1973.

Scripture quotations identified NAS are from the New American Standard Bible, © The Lockman Foundation 1960, 1962, 1963, 1968, 1971, 1972, 1973, 1975, 1977.

Scripture quotations identified NEB are from THE NEW ENGLISH BIBLE. Copyright © The Delegates of the Oxford University Press and the Syndics of the Cambridge University Press 1961, 1970. Reprinted by permission.

Poem on page 108 is from A TIME FOR GIVING by Jill Briscoe, Copyright © 1979 by Ideals Publishing Corporation. Reprinted by permission.

Library of Congress Cataloging in Publication Data
Briscoe, Jill.
    Queen of hearts.
    1. Women—Religious life. 2. Bible. O.T. Proverbs
XXXI, 10–31—Criticism, interpretation, etc. I. Title.
BV4527.B73   1984   248.8′43   83–21253
ISBN 0–8007–1387–7

TO
the many
virtuous women
I have been privileged
to know,
who have brought
a touch of Jesus
to my life

WORKSHEETS

The worksheets in this book have
been designed to
facilitate review and
application of the
chapter material.
They can be used for Sunday school, campus
situations, home Bible-study groups, or adapted for
individual devotions.

CONTENTS

Preface

PREFACE

How can I do it all? Be the woman God wants me to be; my husband adores; my children demand; my boss requires; my friends depend on.

The Proverbs 31 woman has long stood as the Statue of Liberty—at the harbor of the City of Womanhood, welcoming all who flee from being anything less than perfect.

But what if I have runs in my stockings (I'm sure they were all right when I left home); consistently lose one of my husband's socks in the washing machine; and regularly misplace my car in the supermarket parking lot *(it's blue, sir—I know it's blue!)?*

Is there any hope for me if I dream of writing a book about my small children called *From Here to Insanity?*— and if I am shaped like a pillow instead of a post? Do I have to perform to please; compete to catch a man and keep him—or can I stay single and dare to like it?

God's Queen of Hearts will help me to find out how to be the best that I can be—not a woman who is "perfectly becoming" but a woman who is "becoming perfect" little by little and day by day!

JILL BRISCOE

QUEEN OF
HEARTS

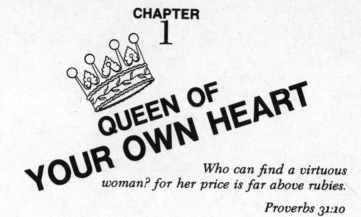

CHAPTER
1

QUEEN OF
YOUR OWN HEART

*Who can find a virtuous
woman? for her price is far above rubies.*

Proverbs 31:10

Where Do I Begin?

WOULDN'T YOU LIKE TO BE A QUEEN OF HEARTS?
Queen of your husband's heart, your children's hearts,
your servants' and the merchants' hearts? Wouldn't you
really like to care about those less fortunate than yourself?
And what about God? Who wouldn't want to be Queen of
His heart? Maybe some of us would settle for one of the
above or, perhaps, if honest, *none* of the above! We've
taken all we're going to take; we've given all we're going
to give—and it hasn't worked.

Let me introduce you to Scripture's maddening model,
this "Bionic Christian Woman" who lives in Proverbs 31.

She is willing to be transparent, inviting us to walk into
her life, kick off our shoes, and make ourselves at home,
as we investigate how she made it all happen. Her wonderful world apparently worked perfectly, giving us a
gleam of hope that things could work out for us as well.

*Who can find a virtuous woman? for her
price is far above rubies.*

The heart of her husband doth safely trust in her, so that he shall have no need of spoil.

She will do him good and not evil all the days of her life.

She seeketh wool, and flax, and worketh willingly with her hands.

She is like the merchants' ships; she bringeth her food from afar.

She riseth also while it is yet night, and giveth meat to her household, and a portion to her maidens.

She considereth a field, and buyeth it: with the fruit of her hands she planteth a vineyard.

She girdeth her loins with strength, and strengtheneth her arms.

She perceiveth that her merchandise is good: her candle goeth not out by night.

She layeth her hands to the spindle, and her hands hold the distaff.

She stretcheth out her hand to the poor; yea, she reacheth forth her hands to the needy.

She is not afraid of the snow for her household: for all her household are clothed with scarlet.

She maketh herself coverings of tapestry; her clothing is silk and purple.

Her husband is known in the gates, when he sitteth among the elders of the land.

She maketh fine linen, and selleth it; and delivereth girdles unto the merchant.

Strength and honour are her clothing; and she shall rejoice in time to come.

> *She openeth her mouth with wisdom; and in her tongue is the law of kindness.*
>
> *She looketh well to the ways of her household, and eateth not the bread of idleness.*
>
> *Her children arise up, and call her blessed; her husband also, and he praiseth her.*
>
> *Many daughters have done virtuously, but thou excellest them all.*
>
> *Favour is deceitful, and beauty is vain: but a woman that feareth the Lord, she shall be praised.*
>
> *Give her of the fruit of her hands; and let her own works praise her in the gates.*

Verses 10–31

At this point, let me explain that this "perfect woman" never really existed at all—save in the hopes and dreams of a real-life queen! We are looking at some royal advice given by a royal lady who bore a royal son called Lemuel. But no matter that the woman she so graphically describes didn't live at all, she serves as an example, not only for King Lemuel, but also for you and for me. We do not find her sitting in the rubble of her relationships, but rather praised by all who knew her for her vibrant virtue, her noble character. She appears to be a very together person.

"That's all very well," you may say, "but where do *I* begin?"

You begin with yourself!

A Good Self-Image

Being a queen of your own heart means you have a realistic appraisal of yourself. You cannot only laugh at the future, and grin at the past, you can learn to chuckle at the present, too. Once you can laugh not only at the past, present, and future, but also at yourself, you have begun to get somewhere. The problem is that we all take ourselves far too seriously, wringing our hands about past mistakes we can do absolutely nothing about; peeping fearfully around the corner of tomorrow, wondering what a mess we're going to make of the future, and, ending up being paralyzed with fear about the present and our ability to cope with it all. Our Queen of Hearts could laugh at times to come. She was "not afraid of the snow" either! Cheerfully facing a cold winter, she prepared to take it on. She had confidence in her ability to prepare, to provide, to survive, and to help her family to do the same. When we have a bad self-image, we blame ourselves for everything—even for the weather! We may be basking in the sunshine of summer, yet seeing nothing but the snow of winter. The joy of the present is lost in the dread of the future. We play the "if only" game day and night. *If only* we were married to someone else; if we had another child; if we had less children; if we had *no* children! *If only* we were pretty, intelligent, or social butterflies. *If only* we were gourmet cooks, athletic, good with animals. *If only* we were black, white—pink! *If only* we were anyone else in the whole, wide world but us.

How do you feel about yourself? Before you can begin to be queen of everyone else's heart, you have to be queen of your own! Before you can reach out to others from crippling self-absorption, you have to acquire a liberating attitude of self-acceptance.

Belonging Makes You Feel Cared for on the Inside

You see, if you really believe you're worth nothing, you'll do nothing, be nothing, and feel like nothing on earth. You might even allow yourself to slide into the slimy, self-pity pit, and withdraw from society altogether. The exciting thing about acquiring a right sense of self-worth is that you will find it to be a selfless thing, and practicing such an attitude will endear you to all. So how do you begin to feel worth something, when someone has just rubbed your nose in the dirt? How can you feel good about yourself, when your "friends" have told you they think you're a creep? How can you like yourself, when you've blown it—again? It all has to start with a sense of belonging. When you belong to someone who loves you *as you are,* and not as he wishes you would be, you'll find you've found some firm ground to stand on.

Not long ago I shared a cup of coffee with an elderly woman who had been recently bereaved. I couldn't help noticing the way she looked. While her husband had been alive, she had always dressed appropriately and smartly, but now she had a decidedly tacky appearance. Gently, I asked her about herself.

"I don't feel important anymore," she answered honestly enough. "I don't feel I'm special to anyone. Why, I used to make sure I put on my makeup before breakfast, and always dressed up in time for Harry, coming home from work. But now—why bother? Nobody has to look at me!"

"*I* have to look at you," I replied gently, with a grin. "What's more, your kids have to look at you; your neighbors and the storekeepers have to look at you—the people in your church have to look at you."

"All right," she interrupted me, "but don't you understand—I've lost that 'I'm important because I belong' feeling." She had stopped caring for the outside of her life, because she didn't feel cared for on the inside. Belonging makes you feel cared for on the inside.

I had to admit to my friend that I couldn't understand what it must be like to be a widow, although I have experienced a little of the things she was struggling to explain. My husband has always traveled a great deal, and I know how hard it is to take as much care with my appearance when he is not around to appreciate all my hard work. But I was able to remind my friend that the Bible she believed told her she was very special and important, and that she *did* belong. She was, in fact, of infinite worth because an Infinite God had given His Infinite Son to win her infinite life! That fact alone should make her feel valuable. I pointed out that this is where it all begins. Feeling good about yourself becomes a reality when you realize that God feels good about you. Whether others love you or not, you will never feel you are worth much *until you begin to believe you are worth much to God.*

An Inferiority Complex

When I was a little girl, I had the mistaken idea that my parents loved my sister more than they loved me. It didn't seem one bit fair, but Shirley had had three years' start on me. My folks had had all that extra time to spend with her, and they shared special memories about things that I knew nothing whatsoever about. Why they had had a head start loving each other so it was logical for me to believe I was loved less! I developed a real inferiority complex about my sister. She was so clever at math, so swift on the field hockey team, so pretty in her pajamas! My parents, recognizing my problem, sought to "make up" time and assure me of their great love. They were scrupulously fair, sharing everything perfectly evenly with us, but it didn't seem to help. I had a wonderful mother and father and a fabulous sister, terrific friends (a lot of them), great teachers who encouraged me, a tennis coach who believed in me, and yet, despite it all—I *couldn't* believe that I was quite as important to my parents as my sister, Shirley, was! It was not until I became a committed Christian at the age of eighteen that I experienced an internal sense of value. You see, I came to believe I mattered to God. In fact, I read in the Bible I had mattered so much to Him that He who had but one precious Son sent Him to earth to die on the cross for me. Now I had to be worth *something* for Him to do that. Now I "belonged" to God, and I could start being glad I belonged to me!

Even belonging to a beautiful, loving family cannot bring internal security to the soul. The soul that belongs to God knows the difference.

When I first began to truly believe that I belonged to God and He loved me, I was well on the way to loving myself in the right manner. As a new Christian, I noticed the Scripture commanded a right sense of self-worth. I was to love my neighbors "as I loved myself"—and that was an order.

The New Me

Now I could laugh! Not, I hasten to add, at the sins of my past that had been forgiven, but at the fact that they *had* been forgiven. It was a great, relaxing laugh of relief. God told me He would "remember my sins no more" (*see* Hebrews 8:12), and what He had forgotten I had no right to remember.

Now I could laugh at the future too. "Come, snow, come," I could say. Clothed, we would be in the great, scarlet garments of faith. I could stop tying myself in a knot of "notness" about being the mother to my children or wife to my husband I so desperately wanted to be. I could wait till I got there, knowing He would dress my inadequacy in His capabilities when the time came. Worry about tomorrow that had emptied today of its strength was laughed away. That laugh of faith must have been music to God's ears, and it was certainly a pleasant tune in mine after the dirges of dread I had been used to playing on the turntable of my personality. *Loving my-self,* my "new" self, brought sweet relief, and a straightening out of uptight, twisted, troubled thoughts that plagued me. The experience birthed a poem that expressed how I was feeling:

> *I'm not a knot, Lord, no I'm not.*
> *Well, not at the moment!*
>
> *Keep me untied, Lord,*
> *straighten me out.*
> *Get hold of the frayed ends*
> *hold them securely in place.*
> *Help me lay still in Your*
> *hands while You tease out*
> *the tightness.*
>
> *Tied in tight against myself*
> *twisted over in*
> *knots of notness*
> *I'm no good to You or me*
> *or the people I love!*
>
> *Help me, Lord,*
> *not be a knot!*

Loving Myself Is Not the Same as Being Selfish

Confusion came only when I thought that loving myself was the same thing as being selfish.

Not long after I was converted to Christ, I came across a verse in the Book of Galatians that said: "I am crucified with Christ: nevertheless I live; yet not I, but Christ liveth in me: and the life which I now live in the flesh I live by the faith of the Son of God, who loved me, and gave himself for me" (2:20).

There you are, I said to myself, *"I" is good for nothing. The selfish "I" must die—in fact, God is saying here, "I" has been crucified with Christ.* I discovered, however, this *I* that Paul spoke of can be thought of as the old *I* or the old man (or woman) that I used to be. It is the old, selfish unregenerate *me* he is talking about here. This, I found out, was the person I was before I met Christ, received the Holy Spirit, and was born from above. It was speaking of the self-centered, self-seeking, arrogant "Miss Me" who demanded the world to worship at her feet, and sought the company of those who would pamper and coddle, stroke, and attend to her every whim. This is the way people behave because they are unsure about themselves and need attention to feel of value. And we behave this way, of course, because we are supremely selfish. The Bible in no way tells us to love this ugly part of us, but there can be a *new me,* says the apostle Paul. This is the "new man" (or woman) that lives by the faith of the Son of God. This is the regenerate, changed *me,* for if any man (or woman) be ". . . in Christ, he is a new creature: old things are passed away; behold, all things are become new" (2 Corinthians 5:17). This, then, is the *me* "I" can begin to feel good about! The new *me* who is dressed in Christ lives a new life in a new dimension with a whole new power to be different. Christ sets me free to be the me that God has always wanted me to be. In other words, to be a Christian means I can begin to feel really good about myself to such a degree I can forget myself in loving service for others.

Blessed to Be a Blessing

Being of value to others brings its own sense of self-worth to our souls.

I can well remember the first time I put myself out for other people—really put myself out. I can well remember it because it was such a shock to my system! It hadn't happened before. Some children needed helping. I was student teaching at the time and had no obligation to go the extra mile. Having spent most of my life (up to this point) going half a mile whenever I could get away with it, and by and large, expecting everyone else to go at least five miles for me all the time, I discovered a caring concern within my heart that was quite foreign to my nature. Born of His love, this new affection drove me to action, and I began to allow children in need to invade my off-duty hours. It was inconvenient, an extra load to carry in an already busy schedule, but the extra mile became a normal distance to travel in my busy days. As I became valuable to those youngsters, I became valuable to myself. I could even like this new me that Jesus Christ was helping me to become. I had begun to learn to be unselfish.

I'm So Ugly!

Have you ever noticed how many children struggle with a bad self-image? In her adolescent years, our daughter would, on occasion, stand before the looking glass and say vehemently, "I'm so ugly." Beauty, after all, is in the eye of the beholder, and the adolescent beholder is not often able to convince herself that there is indeed any beauty there to behold. It was not until Judy's wedding day that our daughter finally was able to say, "Today I feel good about myself." On the other hand, our youngest child (how can children be so different?) has always had a very healthy self-image. Taking a self-analysis quiz in school, he looked at the first question, "What do you like about yourself?" and answered briskly and honestly, "Everything!" *Arrogance*, you say. Maybe—or then again, maybe not. Pete never thought much about the matter, being quite content to be the Pete that he is, and consequently has found himself freed from an enervating self-absorption. He has been able to forget himself in outgoing pursuits and easy relationships. That is not to say our daughter has been selfish because she struggled with a bad self-image—not at all. Judy discovered that it takes twice as much effort to serve others when we use up so much nervous energy and reserves, wondering if we are able to do the serving!

Unfair Expectations

There are many, many factors that contribute to a child's suffering from low self-esteem.

Children can have a bad self-image because we give them one, for example, if we are forever comparing them to a sibling that is doing better than they are, or laying our unrealistic expectations on them, or working out our own frustrated dreams through their lives: "I never made quarterback, but there's no reason you shouldn't"; or, "I never had the opportunity to go to college and become a doctor, as I would like to have done, but in this day and age and with your brains, there is no good excuse for you not to go." Then there is a good chance we will finish up with kids, struggling to find out who they really are, so they can be who they really ought to be! The very best thing we can do for our children, of course, is to lead them to Jesus Christ, so they can get their affirmation from Him, and then teach them how to seek His will for their lives according to the gifts and talents He well knows they have, since He is the One who gave them to them in the first place!

Being in a right relationship with God will give our children that marvelously secure sense of belonging, and mean they will have all the potential for a right relationship with themselves, their world, and other people.

Greater Than Cabbages

"But surely if we could just get rid of that old self-conscious nature altogether," I hear some of you say, "we would better serve our Lord! People talk about being emptied of self, so that they can be filled with God. Isn't that what we should be striving to do?"

Well, I don't think it is possible to be emptied of self, because self-awareness is all part of God's gift of person-hood and need not be a selfish thing at all. In fact, it's this human self-consciousness that marks us out from the animals, vegetables, and minerals. It is this very thing about our humanness that points to man as the pinnacle of God's created order.

Look at it this way—as far as I know, cabbages are not aware that they're cabbages, whereas human beings are aware that they're human beings. The Bible teaches us that we are aware of ourselves because God wants us to be. If you took a microphone down to the local cabbage patch, stuck it under the nose of a cabbage plant (as all good reporters are wont to do), and asked, "How do you feel?" the cabbage plant would not reply, "Like cole-slaw," because it cannot talk. It's only a cabbage possessed of cabbage life. Like minerals in the mineral world, it has no sense of being or purpose, no self-consciousness. It does not sit in a cabbage patch saying, "I'm supposed to be something, to do something, to enjoy something." Now I'm sure you're aware we're greater than cabbages, minerals, and even greater than the animals.

"But wait a minute," you argue, "animals have self-awareness." True, animals are greater than cabbages, yet still they are lesser than humans. Animals are aware of their needs and let it be known by wagging their back ends, growling their front ends, and lolloping down the road after another dog! But animals do not have the capacity for a spiritual relationship with God. Man was given dominion over the animal, vegetable, and mineral kingdom because God created man to be superior (Genesis 1:28). Man is made after God's likeness, after His image, and God is superior! Man has an innate awareness that

God created him to be something special, and in this lies his sense of self-importance.

So then man is conscious that there is a reason for his existence, even if he doesn't quite know what it is. Here's an illustration of this.

Excuse Me—Are You Alive?

Years ago, my husband and I used to work in the back streets of our cities finding young people to talk to about God. We could have sat in church, waiting for them to show up, but we would still have been sitting there today if we had done that. We found them in the weirdest places, doing the weirdest things! One night in an extremely smoky, somber place, we sat down next to a young couple who were twined around each other like a grapevine. My husband poked the young man in the ribs and said, "Excuse me, are you alive?" "Of course I am," replied the youngster, somewhat indignantly. "Why?" inquired Stuart, "Why are you alive?" "I don't know," replied the young man, dumping his girl friend unceremoniously on the floor, as he grew interested in the conversation. "What is the purpose of your existence?" insisted Stuart. "I don't have any purpose," the young man answered. "Why do I have to have a purpose?"

Stuart knocked his hand on the table in front of them and asked, "Does this table have a purpose?" "Sure," the boy replied. "Does this chair, this glass?" persisted Stuart. The young man nodded in assent. "Are you greater than the table, the chair, and the glass?" my husband inquired. "Of course. You know I am," retorted the young man.

"Well, now, even though you know you are greater than all these things that have a purpose, you don't seem to have a sense of purpose yourself. Don't you think that is rather strange?"

The boy talked with us way into the night, sharing that

he had been aware of a need to know "who he was and why he was" for a long time, and yet had no one to answer his questions. In the end, he had given up his search for truth. It is this self-awareness, this inner quest for a reason for being, that sets us apart in the universe. We are, in the end, God's creatures in God's world, made by God, for God, and in this realization lies our sense of destiny and self-worth.

Identity Through My Relationships

To find God is only the beginning of finding yourself. There is no question about it, finding God means the start of the divine explanation of who you are; where you are; why you are who you are; why you are where you are! When you have been born again by the Spirit of God, you will probably be able to stand back and look at yourself honestly for the first time, discovering (or rather, confronting) yourself in the light of truth. You will see clearly the mistakes you have made as you searched for your identity and meaning of life.

As I looked back and contemplated eighteen Christless years, I realized I had been looking for meaning to life in all the wrong places. For instance, I had been looking to *people*, searching for my identity within my many relationships. The trouble with this approach was that what happened with others determined how I felt about myself. If my boyfriend disliked me—I disliked me. If my girl friend was rude about the way I did my hair, I agreed with her. God's opinion, if it figured in it at all, was way at the bottom of the heap. Once God found me, however, everything was different. Now what happened between God and me determined how I felt about myself, and other people's opinions were at the bottom of the pile, for a change. This did not mean to say I could care less what folks thought about me; it just meant that my relationships with people stopped controlling my behavior and the way I looked at life in general—and myself in particular. I found out that when self comes home to God and stops wandering the world looking for happiness in relationships with other people who become *his* gods, he finds he's discovered the best about himself. We will like ourselves a whole lot more when we become our own person in our own right, instead of someone else's property to manipulate as they will. It is God who helps us hold our head up high and find self-fulfillment in the discovery of our own personhood.

As the divine explanation continues, we will find out what it means to be created after God's image, an image found chiefly in the fact that man is a unique spiritual and eternal being. As we grasp the meaning of these words, we will discover a whole new concept of ourselves.

Unique Beings

First, we are unique. That means there is only one like us in the whole wide world. We have been handcrafted by the Divine Potter, stamped with the initials of the Master Designer. Stuart and I once had the great opportunity of touring an African game park. One of the fabulous lessons that nature had to teach us had to do with giraffes. Our guide asked us to look very carefully at the patterns on the skins of the animals. "What do you see?" he inquired. We looked long and hard at a group of five animals. Suddenly my observant husband said, "I see every animal's skin is painted with a different pattern. Not one creature is exactly the same as another." Oh, they were all giraffes but each was uniquely made and marked.

So it is with us, I don't mean we are like giraffes, but we're all human beings, each uniquely made and marked, *because we are made in His image,* and He is unique. You can't help feeling special, if you know you are the only one fashioned in such a way. *There is only one me,* you can say to yourself, and begin to be glad about that. "But that is exactly my problem," we wail. We don't like the way God put us together. We don't appreciate the pattern we've been given. And let's face it, few women I know are satisfied with their markings, their height, hair, teeth, or skin, or even their particular personalities! Coming to know God in Christ helps us to realize Someone loves us just the way we are. He likes our height, hair, and even our particular personality! He would not have made us thus if He had not been quite delighted with the finished product. As you get to love Him who patterns you, you actually get to love and accept the pattern!

Spiritual Beings

Second, human beings are spiritual beings because God is spiritual. You and I are capable of enjoying realities of the spirit which satisfy our inner longings in a way material realities never can. We have this capacity because we are made in His image. A young man once said to me, "But I don't believe in spiritual realities. I only believe in the things I can touch and see!" I asked him if he was married, and when he answered in the affirmative, I inquired if the love that he had for his wife was real. "Of course," he replied. "Is your love for your wife a material, visible thing you can touch?" I asked. He got the point.

When I was in my teens, I did not believe I was a spiritual being, or that spiritual realities were realities either, and yet I was interested in spiritual matters. How could this be? *Where do my inquisitive questions concerning spiritual matters spring from?* I wondered. Why should my mind even compute such mystical thoughts if my mind was only a physical piece of protoplasm? And just where had I come by my sense of moral excellence? How did I know what was right and what was wrong, without having to be told? My parents had taught me much that was good, but they hadn't taught me all the rules of life, so how did I somehow know them anyway? And why did I admire the good people and recognize the evil ones? Of course, I know now that spiritual realities are just as real realities as material ones, and are inbuilt into the human psyche to matter more to us than mere inanimate objects. God is Spirit and we, made in His image, know we are spiritual creatures whether we acknowledge that we know it or not!

Eternal Beings

Human beings have the strangest sense that they are going somewhere. There is a self-conscious conviction that we are made to live forever, that we will never die. We know intellectually that death is a grim certainty, and yet which of us can honestly say we are expecting the inevitable news that it is our turn? We all deny in measure the appalling necessity of death. Why is this? It is because we are made after His image and somehow know we are eternal people made to live forever!

And you know that if God created us to live forever, He must have thought us worth the time and trouble. The fact that He wants us to live forever with Him has to bring some sense of self-worth to our minds and our hearts.

Living With Eternity in Mind

As I read Proverbs 31, I see the Queen of Hearts living every day as if her life depended on it—as if it were to be her very last one. She seems truly to be living every moment in the light of eternity.

The lovely lady we have described for us in this chapter of Proverbs certainly exhibited a uniqueness. Who but she could do all these things and still be standing up to take her bow at the end of the day? She certainly has no equal that I know of. But then, she wouldn't have an equal, because *every woman is unique.* Some of us have some of her talents, and some of us have gifts that are not even mentioned here, but that is because all of us are giraffes! Our lovely lady certainly lived her unique life in the light of eternity and in the light of eternity's God. She was a spiritual person. She had a holy awe of the Almighty, a conscious knowledge that she was accountable and responsible for the life that she lived. She was, I am sure, superconscious that while she was serving others, she was serving Him whom she loved supremely.

In fact, if I knew I had but one day left to live, I think I would open that chapter up, lay it in a convenient place, and then seek to make my last day on earth a Proverbs 31 day! The fact that God designed us for an eternal purpose has to help us have a right sense of self-importance. As we grow to know Him better, realizing we are accountable and responsible, the divine explanation will continue to communicate the ongoing purpose He has in mind for our lives, and in the doing of that eternal purpose will lie the sense of completeness we desire.

So whenever we want to feel good about ourselves, about our looks, personalities, gifts, or abilities, we can remind ourselves that we were made after His image and we shall be helped. "I am like God," I can say, "unique, spiritual, and eternal, with a purpose to fulfill"—and that *has* to be good!

The Original Bad Self-Image

Satan, of course, would have us feel badly about who we are, and what we do. He is not named our "adversary" for nothing. He does not want us to discover who we are, where we are, and why we are. It was Satan, in fact, who had the very first bad self-image. In past eternities he was a beautifully created being named Lucifer, who lived in heaven, but he didn't feel good about that. Jesus, who lived in heaven, too, told His disciples on earth that He saw Lucifer thrown out of the heavenly realms when he decided he wanted to be someone he was not created to be. He had been made by God to be a mighty angel. (Isaiah 14:12–14; Luke 10:18). He was not created after the image of God as we were, but rather was made with his own unique personhood, or to be more exact, *angelhood.* There came a time when he decided he wanted to be like someone else. He did not love and accept himself as God loved and accepted him. He was not comfortable to be what he was expected to be and do what he was expected to do; in fact, he was not satisfied with himself at all, and that was the sin that eventually led to Eden's spoiling and our downfall.

One of the things that has helped me to accept myself as God made me has been this very thought: I am like Satan when I am not content with the way I am made or with the purpose that God has for "my being and my doing." That startling thought is enough to straighten me out!

Copycats

This thought helps me to stop copying others. I've always struggled with yearning to be like someone else. When I was young, I worked to be like my beautiful sister, or my vivacious friend. When I became a Christian, I began to want to be like the serene Christian missionaries I would meet, or a successful pastor's wife. But after I had come into that relationship with God through Jesus Christ and the divine explanation began, I started to understand I couldn't be like someone else when I was meant to be like me. To seek to be like someone else was not only stupid, it was sin! We do not see the Queen of Hearts copying anyone. There is no other woman in the text that she is trying to be like. She appears to be content to be true to her own personhood and live outside the bonds of copycat living.

However, to be my own person apart from a submissive attitude to God is sin, too. Becoming happy with myself, so I do not copy others, does not mean I must worship myself. When self becomes god, selfishness is inevitable if I am doing my own thing, regardless of God and His plan for my life. Being "free to be me" in the biblical sense means being free to be the me that God has in mind! Therefore, the divine explanation must continue.

Works of Service

"But," you remonstrate, "how does this divine explanation work? Will I hear a voice from heaven calling out to me, telling me about my gifts and my talents? What is a heavenly call anyway? How can I know what God wants me to do?" I'm glad you asked me that! In the Bible, God has revealed in principle what He wants us to do in practice. It is all clearly written down in His Word. Therefore, we need to be reading the Bible regularly—searching the Scriptures daily. He tells us He has gifted us with spiritual abilities for the works of service He wants us to perform. We are gifted with these spiritual abilities by the Holy Spirit, as soon as He enters our lives. As He comes into our hearts, He brings His gifts with Him. The practical outworking of that principle is very simple. We need to experiment to discover which gifts He has already given us. We will need to volunteer to do some work of service, and in doing it, we shall soon find out if we are gifted or not. So what is a call? It is simply doing the next obvious thing that needs to be done—and doing it with all we have. As we begin to do some work of service for all we are worth, we will begin to feel we are worth something! In fact, we will be able to say, "Thank You, Lord, I am free to be me, the me You made and gifted me to be."

Start Where You Are With What You've Got

For example, I had always wanted to speak and teach. I knew I had some talents in these directions, since I had obtained good grades in school for speech and drama, and enjoyed the classroom as a teacher. But how was I to find out if I had been spiritually gifted to teach the Scriptures? How could I know if God had called me to this ministry? Searching the Bible, I began to underline principles that were relevant to my questions. I read that all followers of Christ were commanded to share their faith, and I must start right where I was, teaching what I knew. As I began to articulate my faith to my friends and neighbors, I discovered the ones and twos I spoke to had relatives and friends they desired me to speak to as well. As they brought them to me, it became a practical necessity for us all to meet together on one night, and so my first Bible class began.

In other words, I took a principle of Scripture that instructed me to start *where I was* with what I had to share, and as I was obedient to that injunction, God blessed, folks were helped, and brought along more people, until one thing began to lead to another. The set of talks I had prepared for the few began to be in demand for the many. I was invited to talk in churches in other towns. I returned to my Bible and discovered the early disciples trained certain gifted men to shepherd new disciples, and since I had a young family and couldn't leave them alone, it became obvious I needed to train leaders, so I could leave them to continue what I had begun.

I prepared some messages for leaders, and upon a certain day, delivered them to seven or eight invited people.

They got very excited about the material, said they would teach it to others, and one of the men asked me if I would go to a local meeting of youth leaders he was in charge of and give the substance of my lectures to their convention. This led to the next step, and the next and the next—and I suddenly became aware that if you start *where you are with what you've got,* are faithful and conscientious doing your homework, and are caring for people, the so-called gift—if it is there—will become an obvious visible reality. The church will then confirm it, and under its authority, put it to work and guide and protect you in the use of it.

"A Call" Is Doing the "Next" Thing

As we look at the Queen of Hearts, we see her stretching out her hands to the needy around her. She started where she was with what she had. Being a woman who feared the Lord, she knew her God was the God of the poor, so she had no difficulty obeying her Master and serving such unfortunate creatures within the scope of her influence. One deed obviously led to another, until her works of service praised her in the city gates. Her gifts became obvious as she volunteered for the works of service she believed she had been called to do, because of her relationship with God.

When at last you find something you can do for God, you begin to like yourself for doing it. We all like to be liked. We all want to be accepted by others for who we are and what we do. We all want to feel good about ourselves as well. When we are rejected by someone else, we tend to reject ourselves. When we come to the realization that we are accepted by God, even when we talk too much, look tacky, or even make fools of ourselves as we learn a job we have never done before, we have an easier time accepting ourselves. And when we are a blessing in someone else's life, and they accept us because of that, or when we eventually slot into the right work of service for the Lord, we're well on the way to experiencing more self-confidence.

The Problem of Conformity

The problem is society has a nasty habit of deciding who is acceptable and who is not. Conformity is the key. Conform and you are *in*, as a rule. Last time I visited England I rode the tube into town. A punk rocker entered the carriage and sat opposite me. I was amazed! Having worked with extraordinary young people from the streets of Europe, I had to admit I had never seen one quite like this one before. His hair was standing up in the middle of his head like cock's comb. It was dyed white, while the sides of his skull up to his hairline were completely shaved. His face resembled a clown's, and he wore painted silver pumps on his feet. I couldn't resist asking him if his friends dressed the same way. "Of course," he retorted, "that's why I do—I don't want to be different!"

I thought that a very strange remark, indeed. The entire railroad carriage was falling off the seats, gawking at the young man. Then I thought of my friends, and realized that that day they would most probably all be wearing preppy blazers, high ruffled blouses with bows and open-toe pumps—just as I was.

We don't want to be different either. Don't we all dress like our group? Of course we do! We all want to be part of the scene—*our* scene. The freeing thing about becoming secure in Christ is that He sets you free to conform or not to conform, only if it is relevant or right.

Pleasing the Church or Pleasing the Lord?

When I became a pastor's wife, I felt very insecure about the whole business. *What does the church expect of me?* I thought frantically. I looked around for a model I could copy. Where was a neat pastor's wife I could seek to emulate? I wanted to conform to the norm, so that the church would accept me. I desperately wanted to please the people, but to conform in this instance would have been to fly in the face of my gifts and abilities. When I eventually discovered a neat pastor's wife I could copy (and it wasn't easy, since we ministered in a community that was largely Roman Catholic, and priests don't have wives), she was quite different from me. She played the piano, sang like a lark, loved ladies' teas and old peoples' homes. I sang like a crow, had only played on the linoleum, hated ladies' teas and old peoples' homes! "Please the Lord, Jill," my husband advised me, as I poured out my complaint in his patient ears. "We're not here to please the church; we're here to please the Lord." That's it, *right there!* Did it mean more to me that I pleased the church or pleased the Lord of the church? He sets us free from controlling, constricting, conformity—to be the person He has created us to be. I do not get the feeling that the Queen of Hearts conformed to society's demands, but simply asked God to help her make the best of herself for Him.

Beauty or Brains?

We do not get many clues to whether the Queen of Hearts was beautiful or not—but I would hazard a guess that she was not pretty at all, because her adoring husband praised her for her spiritual virtues, while musing aloud that "favour is deceitful, and beauty is vain . . ." (verse 30). Perhaps this means she was not a physical beauty. I love Moffatt's translation of that particular verse: "Charms may wane and beauty wither, keep your praise for a wife with brains." I don't believe our lady was a brainy-bump (or a brawny-bump for that matter, although it does say, "She strengtheneth her arms."). Having studied her character, I glean the fact that the Queen of Hearts was the sort of woman who was very happy with what she had and very happy with what she hadn't. I'm sure she did not try to conform to her group to try to be acceptable. She was not a copycat. She didn't need to be. "But," I hear you cry, "what didn't she have? What couldn't she do? She didn't need to be affirmed by a group because she had it all." Not so! She wasn't beautiful, couldn't ride a bike, make English trifle, quote Shakespeare, work a computer, or use a snowblower! She simply made the most of her own personality in her own culture in her own town in her own way. If her family and friends would not accept the best that she could be, I'm sure that that was their problem, not hers. The secret lies in realizing God has put us together for something that He has in mind and accepting that purpose and plan. Accepting yourself as God has made you, and being free from trying to conform, will result in a healthy, natural, unself-consciousness that will leave you free to care about others. You will then find you will be able to reach out of your self-sensitive prison and relax, as you reach your full potential.

Free to Be Me

Becoming ourselves in a biblical sense means freedom. We can begin by saying to the Lord, "Thank You, Lord, for making me free to love Thee." Ours is the choice to meet God, to have our sins forgiven, and to know Jesus loves us and that we are accepted in Him. Knowing God has accepted me as I am, because I've accepted His Son as He is, will lead me to another freedom—a freedom from trying to be someone else. If He loves me just as I am, I can love me too. I can say, "Thank You, God. I am free to be the new creature You've created me to be."

"Just where does this so-called freedom lead to?" you

may want to know. "You talk of serving others, of ministering to people's needs, of caring and counseling and getting involved in a lot of time-consuming activities. That sounds like slavery, not freedom to me." That's a good observation!

It's most amazing that the strange freeness of being a slave of Jesus Christ to serve others *is* freedom. I can't explain it, and it's hard to describe, but being set free from selfishness does not mean being set free to do nothing, to live in a vacuum. Christ told us He had not come to be served, but to serve. He calls us to do the same. As we lose ourselves in the newfound security that submission to the Saviour brings, and as we're able to accept the new "me" we are becoming in Christ, then works of service and sacrificial living naturally follow. But it doesn't *feel* like service and sacrifice, you see! It feels, oh, joy, like *joy,* and after all that's what it is. It's called *the joy of knowing that we do His will.* It's a strange paradox, but in the words of a favorite hymn of mine, it leads us to pray—

Make me a captive, Lord, and then I shall be free;
Force me to render up my sword, and I shall conqueror be.
I sink in life's alarms when by myself I stand;
Imprison me within Thine arms, and strong shall be my
  hand.

My heart is weak and poor until it master find;
It has no spring of action sure, it varies with the wind.
It cannot freely move till Thou hast wrought its chain;
Enslave it with Thy matchless love, and deathless it shall
  reign.

My power is faint and low till I have learned to serve;
It wants the needed fire to glow, it wants the breeze to
  nerve;
It cannot drive the world until itself be driven;

*Its flag can only be unfurled when Thou shalt breathe
from heaven.*

My will is not my own till Thou hast made it Thine;
*If it would reach a monarch's throne, it must its crown
resign;*
It only stands unbent amid the clashing strife,
*When on Thy bosom it has leaned, and found in Thee its
life.*

GEORGE MATHESON

WORKSHEET

Read these points to ponder from chapter 1 and spend five
minutes doing so.

• A good self-image begins with a sense of belonging.

• Belonging makes you feel cared for on the inside.

• Now I belong to God. I can start being glad that now I belong
to me.

• We are of infinite worth because an infinite God has given His
infinite Son to win us infinite life!

• You'll never feel you're worth much, until you begin to
believe you are worth much to God.

• To be a Christian means I can begin to feel really good about
myself to such a degree I can forget myself in loving service
for others.

• Man has an innate awareness that God created him to be
something special, and in this lies his sense of self-importance.

• I found out that when self comes home to God and stops
wandering the world, looking for happiness in relationships
with other people who become his gods, he finds he's
discovered the best thing about himself.

• To seek to be like someone else is not only stupid—it is sin!

- The freeing thing about becoming secure in Christ is that He sets you free to conform or not to conform, only if it is relevant or right.

- Being set free from selfishness does not mean being set free to do nothing, to live in a vacuum. Christ told us He had not come to be served, but to serve. He calls us to do the same.

1. **What About You?**
   a) Write a sentence describing how you feel about yourself.
   b) Write another one about belonging.
   c) Share a childhood experience concerning low self-esteem.
   d) Share how coming to faith in God through Christ has helped you accept yourself.

2. **What About Your Child?**
   a) Discuss factors that can contribute to a child's developing low self-esteem.
   b) What can we do to help?

3. **Give an Explanation.**
   What does the Bible mean when it says we are made in the image of God?

4. **Know Your Gifts and Abilities.**
   a) What sort of gifts and abilities did the Queen of Hearts have?
   b) What sort of gifts do I have?
   c) How do I discover and develop my unique abilities?
   d) How will this help my self-esteem?

5. **Make These Comparisons.**
   a) Give an example of copycat Christianity. Why do we want to conform?
   b) What is the difference between a good self-image and selfishness?

6. **Read Galatians 2:20.**
   a) Discuss the verse.
   b) Share one thing you like about it, one thing you don't like about it!

7. Prayer Time

Pray about all the above or "borrow" my prayer.

Lord, set me free to be like Thee. Help me to
serve, sense Your requirements, be aware of
my uniqueness and the capabilities You have
given to me. Help me to lose my selfish-
selfishness in sacrificial service that leads to a
true sense of self-worth and achievement,
which is only found in the joy of knowing
that I do Thy will. *Amen.*

CHAPTER
2

QUEEN OF HER CHILDREN'S HEARTS

*Her children arise
up, and call her blessed . . .*

Verse 28

WHO DOESN'T WANT TO BE QUEEN OF HER CHIL-
dren's hearts? Those of us blessed with children can't help
but want them to love and appreciate us. But do they?
What sort of a mother does one have to be to win a place
in their affections? The Good Book says, "Lo, children are
an heritage of the Lord. . . . Happy, is the man that hath
his quiver full of them . . ." (Psalms 127:3,5). I have heard
it suggested that since a quiver holds five arrows, five
children are a perfect number. Personally, I think five
children are enough to make any parent quiver! Anyhow,
however many little blessings we have been blessed with,
we can learn much from the model mother of Proverbs 31.

Preparation

Lemuel wrote down the words his mother taught him.
These wise sayings were not King Lemuel's words, they
were his mother's. A mother has the unique privilege of
teaching her children anything she wants to teach them.
Her words can have a huge impact in their lives. In fact,
she is exhorted to "train up a child in the way he should

go . . ." and promised that "when he is old, he will not depart from it" (Proverbs 22:6).

What a unique privilege! Lemuel's mother had a burden about this. The word *oracle* or *prophecy* is used in other places meaning "burden." This mother felt a heavy responsibility to give her son some wise advice. She did not, as many a parent does today, tell her child to listen to everything everyone else believes, and make up his own mind. She wanted to make sure she got to his thought processes first. She was concerned enough to want to feed him as healthy a mental diet as she was able.

Stuart and I have been so helped by the wise advice our mothers gave us. Scarcely a day goes by without one of us quoting one of them, or grinning wryly at each other when a certain situation arises. We know how one of our mothers would have reacted to it. The things our mothers taught us have been fine friends throughout the years.

My mother gave herself unselfishly and unstintingly to us children, happy with the blessed burden of motherhood. The wise advice found in Proverbs 31 sprang from another mother's deep concern for her child as she sought to prepare him for his future.

Prayer

What did this preparation consist of? Prayer, prayer, and more prayer.

"O my son," she says, "whom I have dedicated to the Lord. . ." (verse 2 TLB). Lemuel was "the son of my vows." This phrase immediately brings to mind another child with a very similar name—Samuel. His mother, Hannah, had vowed to the Lord that he would be set aside—for the Lord's service, praying that particular prayer before she ever had a Samuel, and *that* is exactly where it all ought to start. Before the babe is ever bathed in water, he or she should first be bathed in prayer.

Stuart has told me that his mother and father spent a few minutes every night, standing at the side of an empty cot, praying that the child who would soon be born would love the Lord and would grow up to serve Him. I do not believe it is an accident that years later, when that mother and father have long since gone home to heaven, the two boys that slept in that cot are in full-time Christian ministry: one the pastor of a thriving church, the other serving missions. I believe a mother's prayerful vows had a lot to do with that! I don't believe it an accident of fate either, that young Samuel grew up to be a mighty man of God, despite incredible evil influences during his early childhood.

Some time ago, I was moved beyond measure to come across some beautiful words, and though I have no idea where they came from, I wrote them down, so I could remember them and use them to encourage young mothers.

> If thou wouldst have thy child a Samuel or an Augustine, be thyself a Hannah. The child of thy prayers and of thy tears will be in the Lord's time the child of thy praises, thy rejoicings, and thy richest consolation.

Hannah had very little time to model anything for Samuel before he was taken to Shiloh to attend old Eli and his worthless and wicked sons Hophni and Phinehas. It must have been very hard for Hannah to hand over her little boy at such a tender age, but she had done all she was able to do, and it was enough.

Start Early

The first years are by far the most important in a child's development. More is absorbed and learned then than at any other time in the growth process. Hannah knew she had a very short time with her baby, and she made sure she made use of every single moment. If we could but live as if we, too, were to hand over our children to someone else's care at the age of four or five, we would most certainly be careful to say all we could say of importance that could be understood.

The best way to say things to a small child of course is to say them by doing. Before a child can say *kindness,* he can understand the forgiving smile on his mother's face; before he can spell *God,* he can sense his mother's anxiety dissipate as she talks to Someone he cannot even see. Before he can understand the concept of love, he can snuggle near his mother's heart, closed in tight to the solid security of belonging. Samuel knew the difference between his father's gentle touch upon his mother's face and the abusive handling of the women at the temple by the two sons of Eli. Respect for womanhood had been modeled for him by his parents. I'm sure you know that what you *are* shouts so much louder than what you say!

When the time came for Samuel to live with people who were modeling something quite different from the things he was used to, Hannah knew it was going to be all right, for added to the influence of the life that she had lived for him she had her secret weapon of prayer. "For this child I prayed . . ." (1 Samuel 1:27) she reminded Eli, and since the Lord had granted the petition she had asked of Him, she had no reason to believe He would renege on His promises now.

Many reading this book will be single parents. Every so often your children will spend time with their father. Sadly, your little ones may be exposed to a very different life-style from your own. Many young Christian mothers have told me their husbands are living with their girl friends, and they hate to let their children be exposed to all of that. "But what can I do?" they ask despairingly. "Be a Hannah when you have them at home and pray," I tell them. "Think of that godly woman's example and let her encourage you to believe God can keep your children, even when they are surrounded by bad influences." After all, God looked after little Samuel and drew him to Himself.

As Normal as Breathing

So if you have the chance to start early, do it! Start when Mother Briscoe started—before the babe is born. Prepare yourself by praying that you will be the queen of your children's hearts. Perhaps you were not given the opportunity to prepare Christianly for the birth of your baby, because you did not become a committed believer until your family was halfway grown. Start as soon as you can and trust God to restore the years that have been lost.

If you can begin when the children are toddlers, it should be a very easy and natural thing to talk to Jesus about things. Make it as normal as breathing, and not some strange ritual that only belongs to church or bedtime. When the children are very small, concentrate upon the concept of the fatherhood of God, the love of Jesus Christ, and the companionship of the Holy Spirit. Introduce your Friend, the Lord Jesus, to your child as soon as he is old enough to understand what a real friend is.

I remember our Peter's coming to know Jesus as his Friend and Saviour. We were returning to our house after going grocery shopping, and out of the blue my son said to me, "How does Jesus get into my heart?" Driving along, I explained as simply as I knew how that He gets into our hearts when we ask Him to come in, in prayer. "I want to ask Him in right now," Pete announced with great determination! "All right," I answered. Pulling over to the side of the road, we sat very still, and quietly I said a simple prayer that I suggested he copy. It went something like this: "Oh, Jesus, my heart is empty and sad. I have made it feel that way by doing wrong things. Please come in and mend it. Forgive me for often being a naughty boy and making people unhappy. Be my Friend and save me from doing wrong things again. *Amen.*"

I had no idea, at the time, how real an experience that was for that little boy. Apparently it was real enough, as just this week I had occasion to read an application he had submitted to a summer youth mission, which related that particular and precious incident as if it had just happened yesterday, instead of sixteen years ago! Judy and David came to know Christ before they were six years of age, as well, and though all three children have been through some tough and testing years, they have sorted through their questions and have no doubts at all about the validity and reality of their original commitment to Christ at those early ages.

Don't let anyone else have the supreme joy of leading your child to Christ. That is for *you*, Mother! Be a Proverbs 31 Queen of Hearts and forge the closest bond of all —the spiritual bond with your little one. Then, long after you are dead and gone, they may well pick up a pen, as Lemuel did, and write about "the burden of my mother —the words she taught me"!

Keep Going

It's all very well to start off in the flush of young motherhood, or in the euphoria of having just experienced salvation, and tackle your kids with some home truths about God. The problem comes when we have to have a consistent ongoing ministry in their lives. When we have to model godly living day after day, in the face of teething troubles, wet pants, downright lies, temper tantrums, disobedience, bad grades, or perhaps even the use of drugs. *Then we really find out* if we are a Queen of Hearts or not. God may not tell us in so many words what He thinks of our motherhood, but the children won't let us off nearly so easily! "Hey, Mom, you *never* listen to me," complained our six-year-old, while a day later our ten-year-old commented, "Boy, Mom, you sure lose your temper a lot!" "You promised to come and watch me play basketball and then you never showed up," muttered Number Three! Broken promises can lead to broken relationships; indifferent attitudes to indifferent children; angry outbursts to cold hostility. It's relatively easy in the rosy glow of a baptism or a baby dedication to promise to bring up our children in "the nurture and admonition of the Lord," but following through on those promises is another matter altogether!

Bedtime or Badtime

Take bedtime, for instance. Bedtime can be *badtime* or *goodtime.* It's entirely up to us! Once the little rascals are in bed, that can be the end of the hassles with the youngsters and the start of some free time for ourselves. If we are not careful, we can all too easily relate our feelings about that to the child. "Why do you always say *thank goodness,* instead of *good night?*" inquired a perceptive four-year-old of his mother one evening as she tucked him into bed. Bedtime should be talk time, cuddle up and gossip time. It can be a review of the laughs and lumps of the day. It can consist of drying tiny tears or the instilling of hope for a bright new tomorrow. It's "Mommy, listen to my hurt heart" time. It's a discussion of the new fashion trends, or the Super Bowl hopefuls. It's joke time—rough-and-tumble time. Above all, we have to learn it takes time to take time! We can't do this in a hurry. And that goes for when the children reach the teen-age years also. If we don't take time at bedtime, we may never catch the opportunity to talk to our child about drinking, suitable

Christian behavior, their fears and concerns, or the girl or boy they hope they will marry one day. You don't just sit down to have a talk about such things out of the blue! You talk a lot about nothing very much all the time, so that you can capitalize on the opportunity to say something that really matters, as the occasion arises. It's when you are sitting by the fire, drinking hot chocolate, discussing a movie you've all been to see, that a natural discussion may arise as to the doubtful moral values that it portrayed. The things you teach your children are usually taught as you ". . . talk of them when thou sittest in thine house, and when thou walkest by the way, and when thou liest down, and when thou risest up" (Deuteronomy 6:7).

Never Stop

In point of fact, you *never* stop teaching your children! The Queen of Hearts still had her family around her when the children were long grown. Not long ago my recently married daughter came home for a weekend. "What do you want to do?" I asked her, as we reviewed all the possibilities. I expected her to say, "Go shopping, go out to lunch, visit friends, or go to a ball game!" "Talk," she said simply. "Mom, I've missed you so much—let's just light the fire, kick off our shoes, and talk." My heart responded with a glad *"Hello! I did do something right after all,"* and I thought about all the bedtimes with Judy, and how precious and important a place they had had in both of our lives. But the goodtime bedtime didn't start at the age of fifteen, it started at one year of age with fluffy, warm, pink-pajama'd children, bathed and fed, brought down in front of a glowing coal fire to roll on the rug, and be patted and played with, cuddled and coddled, and after a long, unhurried time, slipped back into bed, ready to meet the night in peace. Start early; make a habit of taking time for each other, and when you are old, your children will still be around making time for you.

And then, of course, there will always be the next generation to think about—the grandchildren! And the whole cycle will begin all over again with our own children modeling the "burden" after us.

So what are these all-important words of wisdom we need to share with our children, as we walk by their side in the way? Which Christian concepts should we make sure our teen-agers know about, before they have to make their own far-reaching choices in life?

The Pathway

First of all, there is the choice of a pathway to take. ". . . do not spend your time with women—the royal pathway to destruction," advised Lemuel's queen mother in verse 3 (TLB). A Queen of Hearts shares her burden about the pathway of life that her son will need to choose. Lemuel's mother explained, "There is a way that leads to destruction." This is what happened in the case of Solomon, whose women (especially the foreign ones) managed to steal his heart away from the Lord.

Life is made up of choices, and a child has to know that there are two pathways to choose from. There is a right way to go, and there is a wrong way. Jesus talked about these two paths. He said in Matthew 7:13 that the highway to hell is a broad path, and its gateway is wide enough for all the multitude to enter who choose its easy way. He said the gateway to life is small and the pathway narrow, and only a few ever find it.

Our children need to know that they are answerable to God for the choices they make in life, and they are also responsible for the consequences of those choices. We must tell them they have a decision to make. They can go their own way—the way of wine, women, and song, and self-indulgence—or they can go God's way, which is a way of loving laws and self-control, and a life that brings honor to Him.

They *must* realize their actions have consequences and that God will judge them for those actions.

Some people don't like telling their children about God's judgment, but actually if it is explained correctly, that very fact can give a child a sense of security. *If what I do matters, then what I am matters,* a child muses. A child that is never corrected feels his actions have no consequence whatsoever, and therefore he feels *he* is of no consequence, either. He needs to know he matters. All of us need to know that. There are some marvelous words of advice given to another young man in the Book of Ecclesiastes, chapters 11 and 12. "Be happy, young man, while you are young, and let your heart give you joy in the days of your youth. Follow the ways of your heart and whatever your eyes see, but know that for all these things God will bring you to judgment" (*see* Ecclesiastes 11:9). Yes, a child can be told he is perfectly free to choose, but he must be reminded he *will* be judged for the decisions that he makes out of his free choice. Does your child know this?

The Profession

The Queen of Hearts not only wants her child to choose the right path, but she also wants him to walk along it the right way. She longs for him to live like a king. Our Queen begins with the negatives: "It is not for kings, O Lemuel, it is not for kings . . ." (verse 4). She does get around to the positives, but not before she has drawn up a game plan and laid down some ground rules. Our children need to be told specifically what it is we expect of them. They need some good old-fashioned negatives as well as lots of positives. For example, it is not enough to say, "Be a good girl now," as your daughter sets out on a date; or, "Be in early, won't you?" as your son sets off for a movie. We need to explain what we mean by being good, and give an actual time to be back inside the house.

Have you ever talked through some ground rules on sex with your children? Do they know what is acceptable and compatible with their Christian profession as far as their sexual behavior is concerned? Have you made the opportunity to tell your child, "It's not for Christians, O Lemuel, it's not for Christians to go to drive-in movies, get in the backseat and make out!"

Bob's Rule

When our children were facing such choices, we were greatly helped as parents by having a marvelous couple leading our high-school work. They regularly gave a talk on the Christian view of sex. Our youngsters came home with what came to be known as "Bob's rule." The youth pastor had spelled it out for them. He gave them specifics for their dating behavior. In essence, Bob's rule went like this: "Don't lie down; nothing below the neck; and don't take anything off!" That was pretty graphic, but the kids had it in words. That was a whole lot better than "be a good girl"! The problem with telling our daughters to be good in this day and age is that peer pressure presses them to believe that being good means giving a guy a good time by letting him do anything he wants to do in payment for the date! There is a whole different concept of goodness and badness out there, and our kids need to have our expectations of them down in words of one syllable. Now, I'm very well aware it is awfully hard to talk about things like that with our teens—but talk we must. It is especially dangerous to presume they know these things by osmosis.

When Pete was about thirteen, I was having a rough and tumble with him one night, and I was trying to kiss him good night. He, being a "grown man" was trying to stop me. At last, I sort of succeeded in kissing his neck. "Mom," he squealed, "you've broken Bob's rule!" I was delighted to see he had gotten the message! We parents need the peace of mind of knowing that our children have at least had the boundaries spelled out for them.

We mustn't be afraid of telling our children what time to be in at night, either. Even when we are faced with the angry remonstration, "But, Mom, *none* of my friends have a curfew, and it's so embarrassing to have to leave the party early and ask someone to run me home!" I believe Christian parents need to stick to their guns and answer firmly, "It's not for kings, O Lemuel, it's not for kings!" So, helping our child to choose the royal path, setting him off on his way singing, and teaching him what it means in specifics to live like the king that he is, is all part and parcel of parenting. Children do not have ESP, and it's not a bit of good hauling a child over the coals because he has come in late, when you never got around to telling him how late is late! That's not fair. What is more, it leaves the parent frustrated and the child uncertain—not a good mix when we are trying to build bridges of trust and understanding.

The Partner

Nowhere is advice so vital as in the area of choosing *the* lifetime partner. The right choice is imperative.

If we have managed to set our children off on the right pathway when they are young, and encouraged and guided them in their walk with God, we are halfway there. If they are living like Queens, they stand a good chance of attracting Kings. They will be spending their time with young people of like mind. We can encourage them to choose their friends from among Christians, and that can provide a choosing pattern for their more serious dates.

Then I believe we need to alert our children to the fact that all professed Christians are not always living like kings. There are kings who are living like paupers in the Christian world. Sometimes a boy who does not profess any Christianity whatsoever may treat your child more honorably than a truly born-again person. It is not enough to ask, "Is he a Christian?" We need to ask the deeper question: "What *sort* of a Christian is he?" We must challenge our youngsters to aim high, to reach for a star, to decide to do without a date rather than do with a date without morals.

Maybe there is a huge problem because you are living in a town where there is no vibrant church and no youth group for your children to go to. Therefore there is no choice of good Christian dates for them. What do you do then? What is your answer when your child comes to you and complains, "Mom, I'm the *only* Christian in my class!" I remember one of our children coming home with such a complaint, and I will always remember my husband's cool answer.

Positive Peer Pressure

He explained that peer pressure works both ways, negatively and positively. "You can wail 'I'm the only one, and soon I will be none because this peer pressure is going to be too great for me,' " he said. "Or you can say, 'I'm the first one, and soon there will be lots more of me!' You can make that happen." In our case, that is exactly what occurred.

It took a long time, much effort, lots of money, and a commitment on behalf of us parents to be dedicated to the job of influencing our children's friends for Christ. It took hours of talking, romping, and barbecuing; it took sledding, vacationing, laughter, and tears, but it was eternally well worthwhile because at the end of it all, we had a huge group of excited young Christians who became the nurturing ground for lasting Christian friendships. In some cases, solid love relationships sprang up and resulted in firm Christian marriages. Yes, we can encourage our children to stop saying, "I'm the only one," and start saying, "I'm the first one," and get on with it. We can throw our weight behind the project too, and minister to our friends' children and our children's friends. There are too many parents who fear being a friend to their children's friends. There are others also who simply buy a quarter-barrel of beer for the football team after games and vacate the house for the ensuing party, thinking they are the "coolest" parents in the world! Why aren't we better stewards of our lovely Christian homes and provide pizza and Coke as an alternative to the quarter-barrel binge? What an opportunity to get to know our children's peer group firsthand, and find out what we are up against! Let's look at it positively: what potential princes and princesses we have under our very noses!

"He Wouldn't Be Interested"

David, our son, was just sixteen years of age when the Billy Graham film *Time to Run* came to our town. He was shy and retiring and didn't go around looking for trouble. Stuart had asked him not too long before this incident what his friends thought about the fact that he was a Christian. Dave had answered typically bluntly and honestly, "They don't know, Dad!" They didn't know, because Dave reckoned he knew what was good for him and by far the safest course was not to tell them. "Why don't you ask your friend Larry to the film?" I suggested brightly. "He wouldn't be interested," he replied emphatically. "But, how do you know he wouldn't if you don't even ask him?" I insisted. "Stop pushing me, Mom,"

Dave warned me. "Maybe I'll ask him and maybe I won't —I'll see."

Every day in true pushy fashion I pestered Dave about inviting Larry to that film. In the end I gave up, realizing the more I pushed the more adamant Dave was becoming. I turned to two other Christian parents I knew who were as concerned as I was about the situation at school, and we began to form a prayer chain. We found it far harder praying than saying, but we worked hard at it, taking the children's names and praying over them together once a week. David never did get around to asking Larry, but God heard our prayers and answered in a way that taught Dave and me a lesson we never forgot.

Out of the blue the very last day of the film, Larry said to Dave, "Dave, why don't we go to that film *Time to Run* tonight?" Dave swallowed, hardly able to believe his ears. "Okay," he sputtered. We picked Larry up along with three or four of the other children on our list who had also agreed to come along, and as Larry got into the car he announced, "I'm going to become a Christian tonight! Dave, will you show me how?" I nearly drove straight off the road, and I caught sight of Dave's eyes, as big as saucers. True to his word, Larry went forward at the invitation, and Dave sat by his side as the counselor led him to Christ. That was the start of great things in that group of kids. Larry continued to grow in the Lord and is now working towards full-time Christian service. Dave, having gained confidence, saw many of his friends on his cross-country team come to the Lord. He then went on to a full-time youth ministry, helping other teens to be positive peers and risk losing their friends to gain them forever. *I* learned not to pressure my children beyond their stage of spiritual growth but simply to provide the atmosphere where life could spring up. I discovered you do this best by prayer, an open home and heart, and a supportive role in the youth program of the church.

Trusting God

I found it most difficult as a parent to trust God for my children. How could I be sure my prayers would be answered, and how would I know for certain the children would be safe? I couldn't stand the thought that they would ever be hurt or harmed, and yet I had to face reality and know that Christians aren't exempt from suffering. God does not promise us that we will never know suffering or sorrow if we know Him, and He does not want us to promise our children that either. One of the most helpful verses of Scripture came to me at that period of my life. It was very simple. Jesus said a sparrow doesn't fall without the Father's knowing (see Matthew 10:29). Through that well-known verse, I realized something I had known all along and yet had refused to confront. The verse didn't say a sparrow doesn't fall. It says that a sparrow doesn't fall without the Father's knowledge. Oh, how I wanted God to tell me that none of my little sparrows would ever fall! If only a great big light would shine from heaven and a great big voice would boom across my many apprehensions, assuring me that Christian children would never make mistakes, never get sick, and never do foolish, sinful things. But I knew I would never see that light or hear that voice. God had spoken already in His Son. He had not promised us freedom from the ills that resulted from the Fall, and we would have our share in that fallenness. But—and it was a big BUT—He *did* promise His saving presence in the midst of our troubles and trials.

What parent has not longed to respond in the affirmative when a little one asks, "Mommy, will God keep me safe always?" We need to tell our children that getting hurt is part of being human, but that we can ask God for

His protection, and know that He will hear and answer our prayer on a daily basis if we do our part to be sensible and obedient children. There *will* be times, however, when He allows us to go through hard things for His own good reasons, and the children will be better for knowing that. Perhaps He wants to shape our character or toughen us up, or maybe we shall be able to understand other people better when they go through difficulties that we have already experienced. One thing we and they can know though, is that He will be with us! He will *never* leave us nor forsake us. In *this* we can be confident.

I'm quite sure the very hardest thing for a loving parent is to see his child suffer. We try, and quite rightly so, to save them all the suffering we can. In the end, though, they have to know some of that for themselves. How well have we prepared them for it?

Saving Them the Struggle

How I have longed to save my children their struggles, and yet the only way would be to confine them to a prison of protection. If they would mount up and fly above their world of problems, they will not do it without a struggle, and what is more, they will certainly be colorless characters if they do not experience some heartache. It has been when the going has been tough that I have watched my children grow and stretch to mature dimensions in their faith, and their trust in Him has deepened, as they have experienced the presence of their heavenly Father through their tumbles or turmoil. The color has certainly come into their character, as it does with all of us through tests of faith, and that's all part of growing up, you know.

Our Ultimate Good

We need to trust God to make our children holy and not necessarily ask Him to keep them happy. The Queen of

Hearts rejoiced over the future, knowing that she and her family were in readiness for it. Are we trusting God that whatever the future holds, we are a family that is ready for it? We can be part and parcel of that readying for the future. That is, in fact, what parenting is all about.

One day my husband was explaining Romans 8:28 to someone. He said that when the Bible says, in effect, "All things work together for the good of the one that loves God," it doesn't mean all good things will work for the good of the good! It means that *all* things, including the bad ones, will work together in God's ultimate plan for our ultimate good. It does not mean our *immediate* good, either, but our *ultimate* good. That made a lot of sense to me. I can trust God then, that He will only permit those things to happen to our family—good or bad—that will make us grow in God, and work out for our ultimate good. That takes a lot of pressure off us all.

Choosing Right

One very practical thing we can do for our children's protection is to be fussy over the type of partners they do eventually choose. Teaching them to choose right in their early dating years may save them years of grief and a bad marriage.

We told our children we would prefer them not to date non-Christians. Stuart stood up on a chair and invited Pete to pull him down. He showed him it was much easier to pull him off that chair than it was for him (Stuart) to pull Pete up. We told our children that if they did date non-Christians, we would suggest they date them only once or twice, and that they should try to influence them for Christ. "See if they would be interested to come to church," we suggested. We taught them to pray that God would keep the partner of His choice for them, and that they needed to keep themselves pure for the right one who would come along at the right time. We discussed their dream mate (and had lots of fun with that one, trying to encourage good desires, and showing them where their expectations were worldly or unfair).

We taught that God said singleness was a gift, and that they needed to accept it from God, enjoy it, and then explore its grand possibilities, because in all probability God would add a gift of marriage at a later date. We encouraged them not to get too intense too soon and to try and have lots and lots of friends of the opposite sex without having to date them. We told them they would be long time married, so it was worth taking it easy, and we tried to share our own love with them and make them want a relationship like Mom and Dad had! We were always superconscious the children felt good about it, when they heard Stuart and me tell each other we loved each other, and that they felt insecure and worried if they ever sensed we were at variance. They were watching us closely! They desperately wanted our marriage to work. What a challenge, and I would add, a joy, to present our message in full technicolor! When God is allowed to choose our partners for us it's right—it's good—it's beautiful—and it can make children want that for themselves.

We can learn some good things to pass on to our children when we read the queen's advice to Lemuel concerning the type of girl she suggested he seek for his bride.

Take Your Time

First of all, she told him to take his time. "Who can find her?" the queen asked (*see* verse 10). It would take a lot of searching to find a girl with such sterling qualities as the girl she had described. One of the hardest things to get over to our teen-agers these days is to tell them that they have plenty of time. "Marry in haste, repent at leisure" the saying goes, but I have heard mothers panicking because their children weren't dating seriously by the time they were eighteen! Some couples marry so quickly they spend the first year of adjustment going through hassles the dating time should have taken care of.

A Woman That Fears the Lord

"Make sure you search for a woman who fears the Lord," the queen advised Lemuel in verse 30. Choose a Christian wife; look for a girl who knows Jesus Christ, loves His Word, and therefore will be trustworthy, chaste, and personable.

It amazes and worries me that so many parents do not seem to think this is important. You can tell they don't think it a priority when they ask their children what their girl friend or boyfriend is like! More often than not they want to know, "Is she pretty? Is he a jock? What does the father do? What are his prospects? Does she get good grades?" Many of the above are important in varying degrees, but none are as important as the question: "Is she a spiritual girl? Does he love the Lord?" That's the biggy.

Aim High

We can encourage our kids to aim high—not to settle for second best; to look for quality partners, and if they don't find them, to do without—to wait. They need to know what qualities to look for, pray about it, and then leave it in God's hands, and let Him work it out. Now that's pretty hard to do, but it can be done. I remember making a list about the sort of man I would like to marry. After much thought and completing the list, I got down on my knees, and showed it to God, expecting Him to sign it and give it back to me along with the goods. I somehow became aware that He was, in fact, asking me to give Him the list. He wanted me to say, in effect, "It's all right Lord, keep it. If You want to produce such a man that would be super, but if not, that's okay as well!" It was the hardest thing I think I ever did to let go of that list. To let God decide if there was to be such a man for me and trust Him to bring us together was a somewhat risky business. But, oh, the peace of mind once it was done. I well remember kneeling down by my bedside and crying with sheer joy. "Jesus, You can see my heart and You *know* I mean it— Thy will be done!"

For weeks I had been playing games, praying fervently. "Lord, You have my word, I'm willing to stay unmarried," and hoping He would be so impressed with the intensity of my prayer, He'd give me a husband as a reward. But I really wasn't willing at all. He knew it, and I knew it, and the boys I knew knew it too! (They know when you are looking.) There came a time when He knew I meant it, and I knew I meant it, and the boys knew I meant it. What a relief. Now I could wait for my King of Hearts to come looking for me. I didn't need to be hunting anymore. It wasn't very seemly anyway. And the greatest joy was the joy of being able to get on with life without having to manipulate opportunities to be in certain places, so I could meet someone who just might be Mr. Right. If Mr. Right was right, he'd find me, and if he was anything like the guy on my list, he'd want to find me busy serving the Lord, honing my skills, and practicing loving people that no one else loved. I enjoyed nine months of that marvelous freedom before my King of Hearts came along. God must have had that list of mine right by His hand too, when He sent him.

A Guide and Friend

In the end, though, our children must choose for themselves, and we must let them. We can no more pick a wife for our child (if we are living in a Western cul-

ture) than choose their clothes for them after they are
sixteen. At the adult stage, all we can be is a guide and
friend. For after all, a parent's job is to bring their child
up to know and love the Lord, make good decisions, and
then to let them go into the hands of God. Letting go of
course doesn't mean letting go of the relationship—just
the dependency. "Leave and cleave" means just that,
and we parents need to remember it! But if a good base
has been laid at home in the growing years, the strong
foundation will continue sturdy in the grown years. We
shall have the marvelous joy of the loving adult companionship of our children.

Of course, Christ can do that, too, when you come to
Him later in life, and He is allowed to bring His mending
power to bear on broken relationships. He will pick up the
pieces of torn hearts and hem in the rough edges, mending the marriage and turning the hearts of the fathers to
the children and the hearts of the children to the fathers.
Christ can become Lord of the home. He can make hostility melt into trust, and child and parent become one. He
can even make friendship blossom from the hearts of
frostbitten, bitter people. Yes, He can! And He wants to
work with you toward this end. It will take a commitment
to Christ on your part and a life of obedience to His principles, but by God's grace, you can become queen of your
children's hearts.

God is a God who raises the dead, heals the sick, and
brings love where before there was hate. It's never too
late to ask Him to be your miracle-working God. Some of
you I know want to ask Him to start right now. You want
to begin to claim His power in your life and His interven-
tion in your circumstances—but you see, you can't start
claiming anything until He has first claimed you! *Then*
you can start.

So why don't you do that right now! Say, "Lord, forgive
me—invade my heart by Your Spirit; then take me home

to start and be—oh, joy, queen of my children's hearts!
Amen."

WORKSHEET

Read these points to ponder from chapter 2 and spend five
minutes doing so.

- Before the baby is ever bathed in water, he or she should first
be bathed in prayer.

- What you are shouts so much louder than what you say.

- "Talk to Jesus" about things with your children. Make it as
normal as breathing and not some strange ritual that only
belongs to church or bedtime.

- "Bedtime can be badtime or goodtime"—it's entirely up to us.

- It takes time to take time.

- A child that is never corrected feels his actions have no
consequences, and therefore he feels *he* is of no consequence
either. He needs to know he matters.

- It's dangerous to presume our children know things by
osmosis.

- Children will only listen and learn from one that they respect.

- It's not a bit of use saying, "Do as I say," if we don't *do* as we
say as well.

- We must challenge our youngsters to aim high, to reach for
a star, to decide to do without a date rather than do with a date
without morals.

- We need to trust God to make our children holy and not
necessarily ask Him to keep them happy.

- Children desperately want their parents' marriage to work.

- Letting go, of course, doesn't mean letting go of the
relationship—just the dependency.

- He will pick up the pieces of torn hearts and hem in the rough
edges, mending the marriage and turning the hearts of the

fathers to the children and the hearts of the children to the fathers. Christ can become Lord of the home.

1. **Caring Concerns—Preparation and Prayer**
   a) If we have come to Christ "late" as parents, what can we do to catch up?
   b) What practical ideas could Grandma or other Christian relatives think of to do to help?
   c) Share problems you encounter when praying for your children (and some promises too).

2. **Caring Concepts—a Path, a Profession, a Partner**
   a) Do you know how to lead a child to Christ?
   b) Do you think it is enough if a child simply attends church?
   c) What can we do to excite our children with the concept of Christianity?
   d) Share something from the study you have learned about helping a young person choose a partner.

3. **Caring Children**
   a) All things being equal, cared-for children will eventually care for us. What helpful advice, encouragement, or Scripture could you give to someone who has not found this to be the case?
   b) Share one thing from the Proverbs 31 passage that you learned about the Queen of Hearts with her children that you would like to emulate.

4. **Prayer Time**
   Take one of these sections and pray about it in pairs or in a large group.

CHAPTER
3

QUEEN OF HER HUSBAND'S HEART

Who can find a virtuous woman? for her price is far above rubies. The heart of her husband doth safely trust in her, so that he shall have no need of spoil. She will do him good and not evil all the days of her life.

Verses 10,11

WHO IMAGINES ANY MAN SEARCHES THE WORLD for a woman who will break his heart? Have you ever heard of a situation where a boyfriend says to his girl friend, "Please tear this heart of mine into shreds for me. Dangle it over the fickle fancies of your unfair expectations; play with it; manipulate it; break it for me, sweetheart!"

A Queen of Hearts has the sense to know that a man needs a woman he can trust with his heart.

"The heart of her husband doth safely trust in her. . . ." A virtuous woman will do her man "good and not evil all the days of her life" (verses 11,12). Without the vital concepts of mutual commitment and trust, a marriage relationship will find itself in emotional jeopardy.

Commitment

A Christian woman knows about commitment. She has committed her life to Christ, to His Lordship and commands. One of those commands instructs her to reverence and adapt to her husband—to meet his needs (Ephesians 5:33). King Lemuel's mother told her son that a man who had a wife who met his needs would "have no need of spoil." In other words, the man would not have to look elsewhere for love, because the queen of his heart would delight in richly satisfying him (verse 11).

"Now, wait a minute," I hear you say. "Are you trying to tell me that in this day and age men are looking around the place for virtuous women? You must work in a different place than I do! Some of us spend our days in a jungle of an office complex, where men make it abundantly plain they are certainly *not* searching the world for virtuous women. In fact, it seems just the opposite is true." And yet, if you ask a man what sort of a woman he wants to settle down and marry, he will almost certainly say, "A woman I can trust." Proverbs 12:4 says, "A worthy wife is her husband's joy and crown; the other kind corrodes his strength and tears down everything he does" (TLB). The King James Version translates this: "She that maketh ashamed is as rottenness in his bones." Now, who in their right mind is excited about rottenness in his bones? What man is on the lookout for the other kind of wife, the one who tears him down in front of all his friends?

A wife is intended to be a crown and not a cross! A virtuous woman will "crown a man's life with blessings." Yes, she will! Even though a man may refuse to admit it, he needs the emotional security that the sort of woman I am describing will bring to his marriage.

I am not saying that if a woman is faithful and reliable, trustworthy and dependable, the man will never leave her. Alas, experience all too often shows the contrary. But if he does reject or abandon her, a Queen of Hearts can live with the knowledge that she did her part. In the end, she is only responsible for her own behavior—not her husband's. God calls us to be faithful to each other, but that does not always guarantee the success of our relationships; after all, it takes two to keep the promises of wedlock. But here, at the moment, we are concerned with the wife's perspective.

Fidelity. First, a Queen of Hearts can be trusted, out of sight. Proverbs 3:16,24 tells us our Queen was out of sight much of the time. She was out and about amongst men, namely merchants and brokers, throughout her working day. This lady was apparently very much a woman in a man's world. She had plenty of opportunity to be unfaithful, but the "heart of her husband safely trusted in her" (*see* verse 11). Second Peter 2:14 talks of people having "eyes full of adultery," and all of us who are part of our world at all, would have to attest to having met people like that.

A woman knows perfectly well how to let it be known she is vulnerable, available, and reachable. She also knows perfectly well how to let it be known she is not. Proverbs 31:25 tells us "strength and honour" were our lady's clothing. Christ gives us the strength to look a man full in the eyes (and not under our eyelashes), and let him know we are clothed with honor. We can even choose our physical dress with this principle in mind. I think of beautiful Bathsheba, who knew perfectly well how to let it be known to the man next door that she was vulnerable, available, and reachable! Strength and honor were certainly not in her wardrobe that fatal afternoon—in fact, she dispensed with her clothes altogether and got on with the business of having "eyes full of adultery." I know her husband was out of town, and she was lonely, but she knew better—and anyway loneliness does not give us permission to be promiscuous!

Temptation gives us an opportunity to do the right thing as well as the wrong thing. Bathsheba did not need to take her bath in full view of King David. It was just as well that her poor husband, who was far away at the battlefront, never lived to find out he could not trust Bathsheba with his heart! A man needs to know however long he leaves us alone, we are alone; that while he is running around, we are not running around! The Queen of Hearts certainly knew what it was to be alone, but she used that time for productive pursuits and didn't gamble with her marriage.

There seems to have been a great sense of mature trust and respect between herself and her husband. They obviously gave each other space to grow and room to breathe on the basis of the commitment that had been made. A lifetime commitment to do each other "good and not evil —all the days of our lives" is the place to start.

Next time an opportunity comes to be a virtuous wife or "the other kind," remember you are not the first person to have ever been tempted in this respect. First Corinthians 10:13 tells us, "There hath no temptation taken you but such as is common to man: but God is faithful, who will not suffer you to be tempted above that ye are able, but will with the temptation also make a way to escape, that ye may be able to bear it." Call to mind that you are being given a chance to do the right thing just as surely as the wrong. An old Chinese proverb says, "You can't stop the birds from flying over your head, but you *can* stop them from nesting in your hair!" There are ways of letting the person in question know we are our husband's Queen of Hearts. We don't need to respond to the look, laugh at the joke, or agree by our shy silence with the sly disparagement of Christian values we hold dear. We can let it be known whose we are and whom we serve. Our husbands need to know we will be doing that as the occasion arises!

Sexuality. Second, a husband is looking for a woman with a healthy view of her own sexuality. This woman will give a man the emotional stability he looks for. The Queen of Hearts richly satisfies her man, so that "he has no need of spoil" (*see* verse 11). This verse has a sexual connotation. The Queen of Hearts will be happy with her own sexuality and therefore able to make her husband happy with it, too. She will keep her sexuality for him alone and not for his friends and neighbors! However, she will not be a sexless prude, or use sex as a weapon, but rather use her body to bless.

Sometimes it is hard to bring a right view of sexuality into our marriage relationship, because we have learned sex the hard way. Maybe we got the so-called facts in our preteen years, as we listened to dirty jokes on the school bus, or we may have fed loose and perverse sexual mores into our minds with piles of junk novels, popular gossip glossies, or by a constant diet of soap (enough to make anyone sick!). Maybe we have been victims of unpleasant or downright frightening sexual fantasies that we have never sought help with. Some of us may even have had to grapple with sexual abuse in our childhood. All of these things and many others too numerous to mention can make us connect sex with evil, dirt, wrongdoing, and forbidden feelings of pleasure. And yet in the first place, sex was God's idea! It was His *good* idea, too, for what other sorts of ideas could God ever have? The Christian believes that and knows the Bible says that "marriage is honourable . . . and the bed undefiled . . ." (Hebrews 13:4).

God made us sexual beings in the fullest sense, intending sex to be enjoyed within the confines and safety of the marriage union. He placed rules around our sexual activity to keep it sweet. He intended it to be an expression of our total commitment to each other, part of an ongoing discovery and sharing of all that we have and are. True sexual love, as God intended it to be, asks the question,

"How can *I* best satisfy *you?*" while false sexual love asks, "How can *you* best satisfy *me?*" It is the difference between love and lust, giving and getting, touching or taking. The Greeks used the word *eros* when describing the sensual side of love. The problem is, as C. S. Lewis in *The Four Loves* so succinctly puts it, "Eros is the most fickle of our loves." Feelings come and feelings go, and no one is saying that feelings are unimportant, but a relationship based on feelings alone is bound to wax and wane as emotions ebb and flow and therefore needs to be committed to God's authority and control. If God is the God of all of our loves, *eros* included, He will help us to have a healthy attitude towards sex, and help us to know what it is to be our husband's Queen of Hearts and richly satisfy his needs so that he will have no need of spoil!

Dependability. Third, we need to develop an attitude and habit of dependability if we would be our husband's Queen of Hearts. "She will do him good and not evil *all the days of her life.*"

How can a man have the confidence to trust a woman with his heart "just for a time"? How can he give himself fully to a woman with the sense that there is not a corresponding commitment? He will be unsure, hold back, and will not put his heart and soul into the relationship if he suspects the marriage is only a trial run.

In my time, couples got married believing it was for keeps. "Till death us do part" said it all. But today is today, and it is not my time anymore. Now our young people live in a society that is littered with shattered marriages, broken promises, with case upon ugly case of man and wife picking and clawing each other to death all the way into the divorce courts. Now our children stand in front of the altar and hesitate to say, "Till death us do part," save in word only. More often than not they are thinking, *Till divorce us do part.* Guiltily and secretly they are saying to themselves, *If it doesn't work out, there's always divorce!*

Until people enter the marriage relationship without the option-out clause in their thinking, the relationship has little chance of a lasting stability. The reliability factor isn't there. The Queen of Hearts operated on an "all the days of our life" philosophy. The text doesn't say, "Some of the days of her life"; or on "birthdays and anniversaries"; or even "most" of the days of her life. It says, *"All* the days." If we could wake up each morning and look at our mates with that little phrase on our lips, we would have begun to *think* commitment, and would have started to build that safe, sure, anchor word into the warp and woof of our marriage relationship. It is the knowledge of *this* certainty that gives the man that "I've come home" feeling when he thinks about his wife. He needs to know one thing—that it's for keeps—that it's for all the days of his life. He needs to hear her say, "That's how it is, and that's how it's going to be!" Whatever else happens from that point on has to be worked out within the perimeters of that promise.

Think about it for a moment. If a man or a woman uses the constant threat, "I'll leave you," to get his/her own way, the results are carnage to caring—destruction to devotion, and the end of trust; and when trust flies out of the window, the marriage usually ends up walking out of the door.

If I would be queen of my husband's heart, I must know what it is to offer him emotional security in these three areas, those of *fidelity, sexuality,* and *dependability.*
Trust. "The heart of her husband doth safely *trust* in her," our text says, and we can glean some clues as to the working out of this commitment from this word *trust.* In the Old Testament the word means "to have faith in," or to "go on believing in," and is used in various forms 152

times, showing us its importance. The rendition of the Hebrew word signifies the following:

1. *To take refuge in*

It is a good rule of Bible study to see where a word is used elsewhere in the Scriptures. Next we need to study the context. We discover our word appropriately enough in a love story. Ruth, a young widow, comes to live in Bethlehem, brought to that place by Naomi, her mother-in-law, who had left her city in a time of famine to live in Moab. Ruth loves Naomi. Her husband and father-in-law have both died in her own land, and now she returns to Bethlehem. In the course of time she meets one of the rich and eligible leaders of the town, who happens to be one of Naomi's relatives. The story reveals a caring God looking after His poverty-stricken children (Ruth and Naomi), but it also shows the respect that Ruth gained in the eyes of Boaz, who has been carefully observing her, and who believes her to be a virtuous woman. He says,

> It hath fully been shewed me, all that thou hast done unto thy mother in law since the death of thine husband: and how thou hast left thy father and thy mother, and the land of thy nativity, and art come unto a people which thou knewest not heretofore. The Lord recompense thy work, and a full reward be given thee of the Lord God of Israel, under whose wings thou art come to *trust*.
>
> Ruth 2:11,12, *italics added*

There is our word and the context gives us the color of it. Ruth has come *home* to Bethlehem, home to Boaz, home to happiness, but all because she has come home to God! She has listened to her mother-in-law, believed Naomi's faith to be the true one, and decided to make

Naomi's God her God (1:16). As Boaz so beautifully puts it, *under His wings Ruth has come to trust.*

She has taken refuge from the harsh realities of life and death under Jehovah's protection. Just like a frightened chick skitters under the protective shelter of its mother's feathers, she has found the warm security of her spiritual homecoming and is content.

I do not think it an accident that the word *trust* that is used here is also used to describe the experience of the King of Hearts with his Queen! The Proverbs 31 husband is a lucky man indeed. He knows he can come home to a woman who will welcome him to the security and spiritual warmth of her heart. He can come in out of the cold and take refuge under her wings. He can come home at the end of the day to "nestle instead of wrestle." There is a sense in which a man needs his woman to be spiritually trustworthy. That doesn't mean his wife is to be the spiritual head of the home. It means he can trust her to be a woman who fears the Lord and is growing in God. She will be a woman who so winsomely delights in the Lord that he will delight in the fact she delights! He knows she will pray for him, believe in him, and that her spiritual growth will only enhance their relationship.

What is more, a spiritually stable wife should be an emotionally stable wife, as well. Our menfolk can well do without opening the front door every evening, wondering what on earth they're going to find on the other side of it! Would you say that you are a spiritually and emotionally stable woman?

2. *To lean on*

The word *trust* is also used in another context. We discover it in the words of King David from Psalms 56:3: "What time I am afraid, I will trust in thee." The story tells us (in 1 Samuel 21:10–15) that David feared for his life. Saul was chasing him about the wilderness, hunting him down like an animal. He could not stay in any one place for very long, and he could not provide for his family as he would like to have done. But David knew he could rely on God and so when he was afraid he *trusted* Him.

Men can be afraid. They can be like David, mighty king and warrior though he was. Today our men are pressured not so much by wicked kings, but by the rat race, or a weak economy. They feel helpless and humiliated, when for no fault of their own, they lose their employment and cannot provide for their families as they should and as they would! It is at such times as these that the King of Hearts needs to know he can lean on his Queen. Will she still believe in him? Will she make do well? Or will she whine because she cannot dine; has to do without a vacation; or has less money than last year to buy the newest fads and fashions? When bad times come, will we threaten our husbands or will we support them? Will we be able to say, "I'm content with such things as I have; take courage for He has said He will not fail us nor forsake us" (*see* Hebrews 13:5)?

Our model Queen was worthy of her King's trust. We read in verse 21, "She is not afraid of the snow for her household. . . ." She had been busy, diligently making provision for the hard times that might lie ahead so "she could rejoice in times to come" (*see* verse 25). In fact, when the "times to come" looked like they were coming, I'm sure the Queen of Hearts welcomed them. The New English Bible says she can "afford to laugh at tomorrow" (verse 25). It is a lucky man indeed, who finds a queen of his heart whom he can *trust,* on whom he can lean in hard times and know she will not collapse under his weight, because she in turn is "leaning on the everlasting arms."

When Stuart and I were working for a youth mission in Europe, we were very adequately cared for, but could not say we enjoyed many luxuries. My husband had left an excellent job with the promise of promotion. He found it very hard not to be able to give us the things he would have been able to provide—if he had stayed in his secular employment and had not ventured into full-time Christian work. Our future was not a little uncertain, and the last thing he needed from me was a nagging refrain about the low budget, the lack of resources, or the holiday we couldn't afford. He needed me to be his Queen of Hearts! He needed to know I knew how to draw my help and satisfaction from the One under whose wings *I had come to trust.* I found out he was very glad to lean on my cheerful attitude. I had to show him I really meant it when I said, "People matter more than things, and people matter more than plans, and we have each other, our beautiful children, a roof over our heads, food in our stomachs, our health, and above all, our love!" He had to know I wasn't just *saying* that; that I was sincere because it was reality in my life.

So, to sum it all up; the word *commitment* means, "For better for worse, for richer for poorer, in sickness and in health, till death us do part." It involves a trust in each other to come through on the promises we made to "God and before these witnesses"—however many years ago we made those promises. It means trusting God and resting 'neath His wings as He nurtures our spiritual life so that we in turn may be a source of refuge and strength to our husbands.

Communication. Next, I believe good communication is imperative, as a couple works out their commitment at a practical level day by day.

If we could listen to our model woman talk, I'm sure we would hear words of wisdom and kindness. The Bible says, "She openeth her mouth with wisdom; and in her tongue is the law of kindness" (verse 26). What man is there who does not wish for a wife who knows what it is to open her mouth and uses her tongue to bless! A Queen of Hearts knows what it is to open her mouth with wisdom!

1. *Wisdom*

"Oh, dear," you moan. "I was afraid of that." My husband has never seen my grades from school, and I've decided he never will. He's so intelligent and I feel so dumb when I compare myself with him. But we are not supposed to compare ourselves with our husbands, or with anyone else for that matter. That's like comparing apples and oranges. We are supposed to be busy learning how to open *our* mouths with wisdom and kindness and not be feeling intimidated by what comes out of *his* mouth.

All Christians can do this, for the "fear of the Lord is the beginning of wisdom . . ." (Psalms 111:10). There is a spiritual wisdom that has nothing to do with intellectual prowess. It comes to those who nurture a meek and quiet spirit, as they nestle under His wings and trust Him to teach them spiritual realities. You don't need a Ph.D. to have something wise to say—you just need to know the Lord.

I knew a girl once who didn't even finish school. She didn't have a very high IQ, and so her brothers were encouraged to go on to higher learning, as the saying goes, while Joan was kept at home to help in the family business. The boys did well, advancing in their careers, made lots of money, bought big homes, yachts, and jewels, and got into a big mess with their family relationships. They did not care about God, and they did not care about each other, either. Joan, on the other hand, loved God. It intrigued me to be in her home on one occasion and hear her father order her to sit down and write a letter to her brothers, rebuking them for their wasteful life-style that was destroying their marriages. "She always knows *how* to say things, so they'll listen," her father told me, in an apologetic manner! Wisdom!

Another time I was there when the phone rang, bringing the shocking news of a terrible accident that took the young life of a near cousin. Without ado, the mother thrust the phone into Joan's hands, crying out, "Talk to them, talk to them—say something!" I listened as Joan, weeping herself, "said something," concerned and compassionate. She couldn't finish school but she was a Queen of Hearts all right. She knew the Lord of Wisdom and borrowed His healing words to great effect.

2. *Interest*

Good communication begins with being interested— interested in everything and everybody. Sometimes Christians think they should only be interested in so-called Christian matters. These sorts of people are not very interesting to talk to.

A woman who fears and reverences the Lord reverences Him for the wonderful world He has made, as well as for the wonderful God that He is. Being a Christian means being interested, not only in the Father, but in the Father's world.

I can vividly recall the week after I gave my life to Christ, someone took me to a meeting and handed me a hymnbook. We sang a hymn I had never heard but will never forget. One of the verses said,

> *Heav'n above is softer blue,*
> *Earth around is sweeter green:*
> *Something lives in every hue*
> *Christless eyes have never seen!*
> *Birds in song His glories show,*
> *Flow'rs with deeper beauties shine,*
> *Since I know, as now I know,*
> *I am His, and He is mine.*
> *Since I know, as now I know,*
> *I am His, and He is mine!*

GEORGE ROBINSON

"It's true, oh it's true," I said out loud—and it was! My world that had been there all the time had taken on a whole new dimension, as I began to explore it with my heavenly Father at my side and as my Guide. A Christian is interested in everything the Father is interested in, and the Father is interested in everything! You have to be interested to be interesting, you see. Practically speaking, all of this leads to good communication. You get so interested you want to share the excitement of your new discoveries. Even men in funny padded uniforms with helmets on their heads can be worth investigation. Yes, they can!

I think the Queen of Hearts would have enjoyed watching Saturday-afternoon football with her husband. Oh, she would probably have sat down with some handwork while she watched, but because she loved her King she would have worked to become interested in the things that interested him.

"We don't talk much," wailed a young wife, troubled about the gulf that was growing between her and her husband. "He never wants to talk about the things *I'm* interested in." Well, try talking to him about *his* interests, I suggested. "But, he's only interested in football," she protested. Surprise him, I said—learn the names of the players on his football team; then leave what you are doing and sit down and *watch* with him—show interest. He will know you are making a big effort and he'll love you for it. He may even begin to communicate with you about the coach or the plays. Initial communication on a lighter level helps to start you talking on a deeper one.

Communication is two way. We must not expect it to be all one way—our way. We need to learn to open our mouths with wisdom, and let the words that come out be governed by the law of kindness. Yes, even a kind word about our husband's football works wonders. Try it. You'll find that he'll like it.

Contentment

When the commitment issue is settled and the interest and communication has begun, contentment will naturally follow. The word *content* is defined in the dictionary: "To satisfy the mind of, to make quiet so as to stop complaint or opposition, satisfaction without examination." A happy acceptance of each other where we are—not where we think we should be—follows the explanation of the other through good communication, and spells *contentment.*

I love the last definition—satisfaction without examination. Imagine a good marriage where there are no suspicions, all trustful days, a supreme gladness of soul that we had all the world to choose from, and we chose right.

Enrichment. The Queen of Hearts richly satisfies her husband's needs, and does him *good.*

Enrichment and enjoyment come from discovering you have married a King or Queen of Hearts. Of course, we can never be absolutely sure we have till we get home after the wedding. I was amused, and not a little challenged, to hear an old Westmorland farmer once remark in a broad country accent, "Ya niver know what ya's got til ya's got em 'haem' and the door shut!" It is in the home, over the breakfast table, in the bathroom, trying to find the cap from the toothpaste, picking the dumped clothes off the bedroom floor, or finding the garage door left open again and again, that we "communicate" who we are. Then we have the opportunity to accept what we cannot change in the other and seek to change what we cannot and need not accept. It is in the home environment that we blossom or wither like leaves on a tree. The unpredictable blessings (or nasty surprises) that emerge when we are at home and slip off the shoes of our character are the things we must work at together. We must divide and conquer. Each must take his share of the work. But that's the fun of it!

One of the greatest challenges for my husband has been to cope with my driving. He tries very hard not to make verbal communication about it, but his rigid body, staring eyes, and clenched fists usually alert me to the problem, and communicate his feelings anyhow! When Stuart drives, it is I who have to bite my tongue to refrain from inquiring if he would like me to get out and help the momentum by pushing! We need to compromise. In our case, I let him drive all the time. The important thing is to get where you are going, expediently and safely, and not arrive huffed and puffed at each other, so the whole evening is spoiled. I also have to admit he really does drive better than I do (slower but better!).

Contentment is satisfaction without examination and suspicion without continually questioning each other's motives. We must look for the everyday opportunities that offer themselves to us to do each other good. Behind every load of dishes that must be washed, every dog that needs feeding or walking (especially in below-zero temperatures), and every garden that needs weeding, lies an opportunity to bless. Whenever a conflict arises a Queen or King of Hearts will ask themselves the question, "How can I do him [or her] good with this one?"

Excitement. People do matter so much more than things, and people matter more than schedules, as well. Oh, how all of us need to remember that. Women who fear the Lord can fall into a trap of being far too intense about spiritual things. Being interested helps, and yet some Christian women fear anything that is not a spiritual exercise. In fact, Christian women can end up being far too spiritual and not at all practical about their religion. I know that has been one of my problems for years. I am a very intense person. I love the Lord, His people, His Church and His work. I enjoy the Bible, praying and preparing sermons, and writing books. I work hard at all of this, getting up early in the morning and retiring late in the evening.

But I notice that our Proverbs 31 Queen of Hearts was a happy woman. "Her children rose up and called her blessed [or happy]" (*see* verse 28), and we hear her "laughing at times to come" (*see* verse 25).

A few years ago, Stuart found me poring over some concordances and Bible dictionaries for some talk or other I had to give, and suggested that I take time out for some cross-country skiing. "Oh, honey, I'd love to but I have to finish this," I replied apologetically. "Jill," he said gently, "you're not much *fun*—you're too busy being so spiritually intense." Oh, that stung me! But he was absolutely right. I sat there after he had left the room, listening to the kids rummaging for skis, and shouting excitedly to each other before they ventured forth into the new seascape of snow that had just fallen. *I wasn't much fun,* Stuart had said. It was true. *In fact,* I mused, *I had almost forgotten that "fun" was legitimate for the Christian.* For years there hadn't been time for it, as Stuart and I had battled through a decade of mission work amongst young people in trouble. I put my books aside and struggled into my winter wear and appeared triumphantly at the family's side. "Mom—great—come on!" shouted the kids, surprised and delighted at my appearance. "I'm glad you've come," Stuart said quietly. "You need to do this for your own sake—as well as ours."

Are you much fun? Is there the enrichment, excitement, and enjoyment, or a tumble in the snow with your family on your calendar? Or are you like I was—so spiritually intense, *fun* has almost become a dirty word?

The King of Hearts sat in the gate attending to the work of the day (verse 23). Some have suggested he was sitting in the gate because he didn't need to go home! After all, his wife was doing all the work and he was hardly needed. Others have commented he was sitting in the gate, rather than being home by the fire, because he knew his wife would be flying round town, busy bringing her food from afar, or selling real estate, so what was the point of coming home to an empty house? We know, of course, that neither of these concepts is correct. He was sitting in the gate because he was part of the leadership of the city. It was in the gate that decisions were made and justice was dispensed. Remember that our Queen of Hearts was married to a prominent leader of her town. He was a man with huge responsibilities who needed some release and relaxation when he did eventually return home at the end of his busy day. I believe he returned to a lot of fun, and that his wife didn't bother too much about dogs and toothpaste, or dirty sandals on her kitchen floor. I believe that people mattered more than things, and that people mattered more than plans. I know she must have made her husband long to be home, where he knew enrichment, excitement, and enjoyment were waiting for him.

Friends. Finally, when I think of contentment, I think of the word *friends*. Tumbling on the heels of that word comes the thought that friends don't have to give answers for everything they do. Possessiveness kills friendship. There must be space to breathe and room to grow. Trust between friends means common goals and interests, and yet the freedom to pursue separate goals, as well. Friends can do the same thing and not compete, and yet can do the separate thing and not be threatened by each other. C. S. Lewis says in *The Four Loves,* "Friendship; it is a relation between men at their highest level of individuality. Two friends delight to be joined by a third, and three by a fourth, if only the newcomer is qualified to become a real friend."

Our daughter fell in love with a tall, blond football player called Greg. He happened to be in the same college, and they met at the beginning of her freshman year. Quite soon they came to a common conclusion that they were meant for each other, but faced four long years till they could marry. So they became "friends." *Eros* had to wait a long time and so was carefully put on the back burner. Friendship blossomed. In Greg's senior year, they decided the time had come for an engagement ring, and our daughter called us to talk about her commitment. "Dad," she asked, "there's only one thing that is bothering me. Can I marry my best friend?" I loved Judy for that question, and I relaxed in the knowledge that this young couple's relationship was to be based upon such a sure and certain foundation—that of fine, fresh friendship, rooted and grounded in their love for God and for each other.

Some of you reading this chapter are saying to yourselves, *But I have tried to be Queen of Hearts to my husband, but he hasn't responded. Perhaps I should leave him, so God can give me a better husband.* Let me sound a note of caution. Many women today, wrestling with a tough marriage relationship, are thinking *escape.* Because of the societal mess around us, they are not just thinking divorce anymore. It is my experience that they are thinking divorce *and* remarriage—and that before they are even free! Perhaps a friend has been released from an impossible marriage situation and now has found a nice Christian man, and is setting off into her second time around. It all looks so inviting and causes those struggling to say, "Why not me?"

Please stop and think. Please wait. Try, if you are still in your marriage, to save it. Put these principles we have been talking about into action and give God a chance to work it out. Wait long enough to see if you can experience a miracle of mending. I know many women who have done this, and God *has* answered prayer. He does work with us for He is committed to saving our marriages. But, if it is indeed too late, and the marriage is over—in every sense of the word—the mate is gone and even remarried perhaps, then consider staying single. Certainly for a long,

long time. And if by chance you are the innocent party and should be facing the opportunity of remarriage, make sure you choose right this time. How will you know? If you get on with being a Queen of Hearts who fears and serves your Lord, you will attract the right sort of man—a King of Hearts, and there *are* such creatures around! I would challenge you to settle for nothing less. In this day and age it is going to take the marriage of a King and Queen of Hearts to survive.

WORKSHEET

Read these points to ponder from chapter 3 and spend five minutes doing so.

- Without the vital concepts of mutual commitment and trust, a marriage will find itself in emotional jeopardy.

- A woman is intended to be her husband's crown and not his cross.

- A woman knows perfectly well how to let it be known she is vulnerable, available, and reachable. She also knows perfectly well how to let it be known she is not.

- Loneliness doesn't give us permission to be promiscuous!

- In the first place, sex was God's idea—His *good* idea. The Christian believes that, and knows the Bible says that "marriage is honourable and the bed undefiled."

- True sexual love, as God intended it to be, asks the question, "How can *I* best satisfy *you*," while false sexual love asks, "How can *you* best satisfy *me*?"

- Until people enter the marriage relationship without the option-out clause in their thinking, the relationship has little chance of a lasting stability.

- A spiritually stable wife should be an emotionally stable wife as well.

- There is a spiritual wisdom that has nothing to do with intellectual prowess. You don't need a Ph.D. to have something wise to say—you just need to know the Lord.

- I think the Queen of Hearts would have enjoyed watching Saturday-afternoon football with her husband.

- The unpredictable blessings, or nasty surprises that emerge when we are at home and slip off the shoes of our character, are the things we must work at together.

- We must look for the everyday opportunities that offer themselves to us to do each other good.

- "You're not much fun," my husband said to me! Are *you?*

- Because of the societal mess around us, they are not just thinking divorce anymore. It is my experience that they are thinking divorce *and* remarriage—and that before they are even free!

- In this day and age it is going to take the marriage of a King and Queen of Hearts to survive.

1. **Commitment—Emotional Security**
   a) The elements that make for emotional security are reliable fidelity and a biblical understanding of our sexuality. List some pressures and influences in our society that oppose those elements.
   b) In twos talk about Ruth and Job's wife (Job 2:9; 19:14,17; Ruth 2:10–12; 3:7–11). What warnings or example do you see in their behavior?

2. **Communication—Intellectual Security**
   a) Do you find it hard being interested in your husband's or other people's interests? If so why?
   b) Do you think you need to try and match your mate intellectually?

3. **Contentment—Social Security**
   a) Ask yourself these questions: *Am I much fun? Do I give people close to me freedom, or do I want to control? Am I a good friend?*

b) Look up a verse about friendship and put it into your own words. Proverbs 14:20; 16:28; 17:9; 17:17; 18:24; 27:6. Matthew 26:50. Mark 5:19. John 15:13–15

4. **Prayer Time**
   a) Pray for insecure marriages that they may be strengthened.
   b) Pray for secure marriages that they may remain so.
   c) Pray for matters arising from this study.

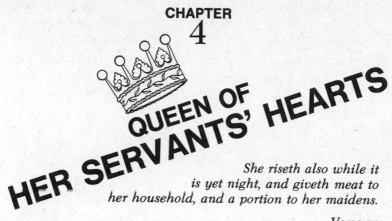

QUEEN OF HER SERVANTS' HEARTS

*She riseth also while it
is yet night, and giveth meat to
her household, and a portion to her maidens.*

Verse 15

A Servant Spirit

USUALLY THE SERVANT SERVES THE MASTER, BUT the Queen of Hearts "riseth also while it is yet night, and giveth meat to her household, and a portion to her maidens." Now that's because she has a servant spirit. For her, service is a joyful way of life, for there is no question about it, she has made a commitment to be a servant of the Lord. I remember the shock it was to my system to learn that once I had become a Christian I had become a servant! After spending eighteen years of my life serving myself, I learned that there were other people in my world. What was more—they were just as important as I was, and did not need to listen to me, as I went around speaking with great authority from the depths of my considerable ignorance! I needed to listen to them, and listening, find a way to serve them.

Following on the heels of that surprising discovery came the confirmation of Scripture. As I avidly read my Bible, I found such verses as 2 Corinthians 5:15: "He died for all, that they which live should not henceforth live unto themselves, but unto him which died for them, and rose again"; and Galatians 5:13, ". . . by love serve one another." David and other writers of such psalms as Psalms 116 and 119 sang about being servants, too, and Paul talked constantly about being a "bond slave of Jesus Christ." Yes, I learned being a disciple definitely meant service!

Authority

The funny thing was, I learned you don't even get off the hook when you are given some position of authority, and have other people serving you! The Bible informed me that even the leaders of the Church were not to "Lord" it over their flock but instead were to be good shepherds, tenderly caring for their charges. Even the *diakonos* from which we get our English word *deacon* means "servant." Jesus put it in a nutshell in Mark 9:35 when He said: "If any man desire to be first, the same shall be last of all, and servant of all."

Now Jesus really could say that because He was Lord of all, yet walked this earth in servant form. Philippians 2:7 tells us, "[He] made himself of no reputation, and took upon him the form of a servant. . . ." In the last days of His life on earth in the upper room "[Jesus] riseth from supper, and laid aside his garments; and took a towel, and girded himself." The disciples—His servants—were embarrassed to see their Master do such a thing, and Peter protested. Jesus, however, silenced him and said, "Know ye what I have done to you? . . . If ye know these things, happy are ye if ye do them" (John 13:4, 12, 17).

Our loving Lord told us that happiness was to be found in following His example and serving others. So many people in this day and age consider this to be a ludicrous concept. The very idea of serving others flies in the face of the constant encouragement we receive from our world to serve ourselves! Self-serving is the name of the game today. In fact, the abundance of leisure time afforded this affluent society has produced a torrent of suggestions from the media as to what to do with all those spare moments. You can go skiing, boating, fishing, or hunting. You can play games, go camping, hiking, or travel to far-off idyllic spots around the globe. Thousands of travel agencies will, in fact, assist you to plan trips to almost anywhere, barring extraterrestrial destinations!

Jesus, however, took a towel, knelt down, and washed His disciples' feet. Remember, this was His leisure time. Here He was at the end of a busy day, relaxing with His friends, and the first thing He did was to take the form of a slave and busy Himself with a menial task. What's more, He told us if we looked for and engaged in such acts of service we would be happy indeed.

What does it take to make you happy? A bigger boat in which to cruise the oceans of the world? A longer pleasure trip to faraway places? More weekend outings to the ball park? Light beer—a few drugs—expensive clothes and jewelry? A better camper or membership in the country club? Try finding some dirty, smelly, sticky, needy feet, and kneeling in the dust of other people's distress, attend to them—then, surprise, surprise—happy you will be!

Yes, Jesus left us an example—and so, incidentally, did the Queen of Hearts.

Think about her for a minute. She was the mistress of the manor, her husband a prominent man in town. She obviously had every opportunity to live a pleasure-seeking life. She had lots of influence, and was highly visible, and I am sure was high on the invitation list for all the important events, too; yet she was in charge of all sorts of charitable ventures, chaired numerous committees, and even exhibited a sweet, servant spirit very early in the morning (oh, how hard *that* is!), getting up before her servants were about in order to cook them their breakfast. No wonder she was queen of her servants' hearts!

Service Begets Service

Have you ever noticed that service stimulates service? When Stuart and I arrived at our Youth Mission headquarters to serve as part of a large team, one impression that struck us both was the servant spirit of our lady boss, Joan. We lived and worked in a large castlelike building that housed up to two hundred people. The building was old and drafty and hard to keep clean. Joan worked on the domestic side of tasks. She was in charge of the feeding, cleaning, and general care of the students because that was what she had chosen to do—even though she was on the board of directors. Now she had taken on a big job. She was responsible for the buying and selling of garden produce, purchasing what was needed for her large family, and selling the surplus from the huge market garden. When the sheep got out of the pasture, she chased them along with all the rest of us. (It usually took all two hundred of us to catch them!) When the ewes lambed too soon, and the little things were threatened by the icy weather, she brought the tiny creatures inside and put them in the hot plate on "low" till she cooked them back to life again. She served high tea and low tea and everything-in-between tea, because that's what you do when you are an English servant. She took her turn at weeding the gardens, washing up the pans, and serving the meals. Late at night you would often find her down on her hands and knees scrubbing the slippery old, kitchen floor as hard as she could.

I tell you, the band of girls who were *her* servants idolized her. Those young women who were from more than a dozen different nations would have done anything for Joan. What they did do was do what she did—they served.

Knowing instinctively that she was not doing all that serving just as an example, but because she was a servant at heart, motivated her staff to model their behavior after her. But whether other people drew alongside to help her or not, she served others simply because she counted herself a disciple—and she believed disciples serve. To have a master who is a servant produces servants who are servants.

Someone Has to Be in Charge

Now there is obviously no point in having masters who *only* serve. That way nothing would get done. No business venture could grow and develop if there was only one person doing the work. Masters are needed to organize and rule. The Scriptures tell us that, clearly, the idea of authority begins and ends with God. He knows us well enough to know we need governors, teachers, and shepherds. We need to know who is the ultimate authority, who *is* boss, so we can be responsible and accountable as we should be.

In Romans 13:1,2 Paul, writing under the inspiration of the Holy Spirit, tells us that "every soul be subject unto the higher powers. For there is no power but of God: the powers that be are ordained of God. Whosoever therefore resisteth the power, resisteth the ordinance of God: and they that resist shall receive to themselves damnation."

In other places in the Bible, wives are exhorted to be subject to their husbands, children to their parents, and servants to their masters. But the husbands, parents, and masters, not to mention church leaders, are also exhorted to be subject to the Lord as they submit one to the other.

Someone certainly has to be in charge—that's obvious —but Christian leaders are ever conscious Someone is in charge of *them* as they are given charge of others—and that has to make a difference.

If I know I have to account to God for my leadership, whether in the home, the workplace, or in the church, I will surely sense a caution in my spirit, as I handle the delicate intricacies of any authority I have been given.

The servants who served alongside the Queen of Hearts knew who was in charge, you can be sure. Her maidens obviously knew what they were supposed to do, and who they were supposed to do it for. Someone had spelled it out for them. The New American Standard Bible renders verse 15 this way: "She . . . gives . . . prescribed tasks to her maids" (*see* verse 15 footnote). The Queen of Hearts gave specific tasks to her servants in order for things to run smoothly, while she was busy outside the home.

This woman had so much going there was no way she could accomplish it all without a happy, healthy staff. When she was away on business, someone had to be left in charge. The choosing of that team, the investing of that authority, required great discernment on her part.

Choosing Right

One of the best ways to avoid problems between staff people is to choose right at the top. You have to know what you are looking for in your leaders.

Think of Jesus. He chose right. He seemed to look right underneath the rough exterior of a person, and that's what we have to learn to do as well. He looked at rough, tough Simon (named "a little stone") and knew He would one day make him into Peter (a rock).

He looked at James and John, and nicknamed them the "Sons of Thunder," yet believed He would see a change as they followed Him. Beloved John would become the Apostle of Love—yes, he would, and all because Jesus knew leadership qualities when He saw them. Do you and I make good choices? Do we know what criteria to use when we are looking for someone to work for us? We have to know what we want. What qualities are the most important? Having been put in the position of having to choose staff over the years, I have worked out some helpful guidelines.

Look for a Christian

First, I have wanted to know, was the person I was hiring a Christian? If I was in the position to choose, I wanted to know that. That was important to me, especially if I was having someone to work in my house. The Queen of Hearts needed people she could leave alone in her home, and I'm sure she looked for spiritual people, too. I needed to know the woman in charge of my children would read my children the right sort of books, help them choose the right television programs, and use the right language in front of them.

Needing someone to help me with the housework when I began to travel, I had to be sure the phone would be answered in a gentle and courteous manner when I wasn't there. People in trouble would be calling and would have to be referred to the right people to help them. There would be secrets that sprang out of our ministry (an important person coming to the house for marriage counseling, for instance), and those secrets would have to be kept. We could not afford to have someone gossip that sort of information all over the world.

So, in effect, I would look for a "servant" of Christian caliber—one who would have sympathy with our hurly-burly life-style and understand what we were trying to accomplish in our work.

Look for Capabilities

Second, I would look for capabilities. It is obviously not enough just to be a Christian. Is the woman capable of doing the job I am asking her to do? That's important, too.

Is she qualified, or perhaps more importantly, able to be developed and trained in certain skills? She must have some discernible ability to come through for me.

Half the job is done when you have discerned where a person's capabilities lie. Are you able to see a raw gift in someone? Then you can take a chance. Jesus looked at a whole bunch of Galilean fishermen and said, "From henceforth you will catch men." He discerned abilities they could not imagine in themselves. Did Peter realize he would be a preacher that would keep a crowd of three thousand people spellbound on the Day of Pentecost? Did Saul, the true-blue Jew ever dream he would become the Apostle to the Gentiles? Jesus knew the dormant possibilities, because He knows all things, and the delightful truth about the matter is He will lend us His discerning Spirit so we can know, too.

Sometimes a period of probation helps. When we needed an *au pair* girl (mother's helper) to live with us and help us to care for our children, we would ask Joan, our senior missionary, to help us. She worked with the girls at the Youth Center on a daily basis and would ask different students to look after her own children for a short time. Then she would watch them carefully. "Time will tell," she would say. Many a time she would recommend girls to me who were not nearly as "qualified" as others, where college credits were concerned, but had exhibited the raw ability to do the job. *Gift* became evident as Joan's children responded to certain girls, as they worked and played together. She would then recommend those young women to me, and I would take a chance and go with the so-called unqualified ones. Most times it paid off.

Look for Caring Attitude

I learned that attitude is everything—or nearly everything. It's not even enough just to have a Christian working for you. What sort of a Christian is she? Does she have a servant spirit, or a snappy spirit? You can have an older and highly qualified Christian nursemaid who is, however, bitter and resentful and busy working out her many frustrations on your children; or, on the other hand, you can have a loving Christian teen-ager who, perhaps, is very young, comes from a big family, adores kids, and is willing to try to please. Which would you pick? Remember, children don't create attitudes—they reveal them, so try to observe the way a woman is with your youngsters when the little imps are being really obnoxious. One of the best things where child care is concerned is to have a trial period, if possible. This way both of you will see if it is going to work out.

What is the servant willing to do, for example? I believe a Christian servant should be willing to do anything *I* am willing to do. Is the attitude "How little can I get away with?" or, "How much can I accomplish?" Does the lady cleaning your house say, "Don't expect me to do any of the dirty jobs," or does she say, "Look here, if you're in a bind and it has to be done, I'll certainly help you out"? Does the clock get watched or can you expect the flexing of time?

Do they care? Really care? That's really important. Do they care about your children as people and not as work load? Are they cutting corners as soon as you are out of sight?

Look for Common Sense

Then I have to ask, does this woman, this teen-ager, this servant, have any common sense? Capabilities are nice, of course, and a caring attitude essential, but a good dose of common sense makes up for a lot!

What does a servant do when the mistress is gone, and the dog bites the baby? Spend half an hour tying up the dog, before seeing to the child? (It happened!)

What does a baby-sitter do when a toddler swallows a bottle of aspirin? Tuck him up in bed, so he can sleep it off (it happened), or call the ambulance?

Yes, common sense counts for a lot. A Queen of Hearts knows what she needs when she starts to put her team together. She looks for Christian character, caring concern, and capabilities, whether raw or trained, laced with a good dose of common sense.

Look for Compassion

But what about the question of taking risks when you're trying to choose right? I think of the poor and needy people the Queen of Hearts ministered to. I'm quite sure she came across people she could help by taking them into her home and giving them a job. Isn't that taking a risk? Oh, yes—but I believe that sometimes it has to be done! It's called *compassion.* And what better act could we perform, than provide employment for the unemployed?

It carries all sorts of dangers but also all sorts of rewards, and only a Queen of Hearts who fears the Lord would even risk it.

I can think of hundreds of stories to illustrate this. When you have been involved in a youth work for over twelve years, there is no lack of material to draw on!

Graham

I think of a boy we picked up one night as we contacted some wild and woolly characters that hung around on the seafront near our home. One of the Bible students turned up with him the next morning, introduced him to our senior missionary, who took one look at him and suggested he be taken to the rescue mission. Graham, the student who had found him on the seafront and had spent half the night talking to him, pled for clemency. "Let's give him a job, sir," he begged. "Please—he can live with me!" Against his better (and as it turned out, his right) judgment, the boss allowed it. Within a week the boy took off with Graham's bike! Graham was unable to give chase, however, as his protégé was also wearing his trousers! You live and learn. There is the other side of the coin, however. Graham, who had had a wild and woolly background, himself, had been given a job at the Center, responded, took fifteen years to educate himself, and finished up running the youth work I had been responsible for. You live and learn. You take the risks, even when you know it could hurt you, because it just might be the saving of a life. After all, Jesus even gave Judas a job, and that knowing that he wasn't going to make it. He never gave up on him, even calling him "friend" when he came to betray Him! Sometimes the compassionate risk is taken and it doesn't work out. Other times, there are the Grahams of this world that make it all worthwhile.

So, to sum up, choosing right involves having criteria to choose by. If we are fortunate, we can choose a capable, caring, commonsense Christian. Sometimes compassion must have her way, swaying our decisions, because God can change men and women, and many need only the opportunity to be in a Christian environment in order to blossom like a rose. A Queen of Hearts stretches out her hands to such people, and reaches into their misfortune to gather them into the warmth of her love. However, once employed, she lets it be known—lovingly—just who is in charge!

Control

Leaders lead, bosses boss, masters master—yes, they do. To make it work though, we have to have the response of faithful followers.

Reading a penetrating magazine article some time ago

on the subject of leadership, I was struck by the comment that in this country we do not have as much a crisis of leadership as we do a crisis of followship. The import of the writer's argument was that we have produced such a cult of individuality, at the expense of the corporate well-being of society, that if authoritative leadership infringes on our selfish individualistic goals, no one is willing to follow anyone anymore! And yet all of us would probably agree society cannot go anywhere unless we have both leaders and followers.

Perhaps it is the good spirit of strong leadership that is lacking. It's *how* the control is administrated that makes the difference to the way the followers follow. And yet there has to be a strong lead to provoke a strong response to a venture.

Character

Moffatt says of the Queen of Hearts, "Strong and secure is her position. . . ." "Strength and dignity are her clothing" (NAS).

She was a strong cookie, that was for sure. But it was not brute strength we read about here. It was gentle, winsome strength. It was a capable woman who was a born leader, knowing how to be strong in a dignified way, forceful but feminine. Those of us with powerful personalities need tempering with the Spirit's grace. I have had to learn the hard way that domination isn't leadership. Paul speaks to this when he says to the infant Church, "We are not trying to dominate you or your faith" (*see* 2 Corinthians 1:24). The great apostle knew that the servant spirit was a meek spirit, and a spirit people delighted to follow.

"But wait a minute," you say. "You've just told me I have to be strong if I am to be queen of my servants' hearts. How can I be strong and meek at the same time?"

Meekness

I think our problem lies in our understanding of the work *meek.* We think meekness means weakness, and that's just not true.

Meekness is another of our English words that has lost its original meaning. When Jesus said, "Blessed are the meek," He couldn't have meant weak, because He went on to say that those with such a spirit should inherit the earth (*see* Matthew 5:5). There is a controlled strength that the Bible teaches can be the portion of those who lead, so that they will inherit their particular piece of earth as a sphere of influence and responsibility.

Jesus was talking about God control, which leads to self-control, which leads to leadership control that does not dominate or manipulate but has a gentle, sweet authority all of its own, one that people will respect and honor. In other words, if God dominates me, I won't dominate other people. I will gain their respect in such a way they will *want* to follow my lead.

Handling Power

How do *you* handle power? How do I? All of us have some power and authority over other people. Every mother inherits her home and rules there. How does a mother handle the authority she has over her children, for example. Does she deal with it with strength and dignity like a true Queen of Hearts? The word *meekness* has the connotation of something totally wild that has been tamed. The meaning of the word is something akin to a wild horse that has been bridled—a harnessed horse, in fact. There has to be a sense of control about our lives if we are to win the respect of those we expect to follow our orders. People simply do not respect people who have lost control of themselves. Kids soon lose respect for their mommy if she is always exploding in uncontrollable fits of temper at the slightest little thing. Children are not going to want to obey a mother like that.

Jesus Christ

When I think of Jesus, I think of His strong dignity, of eternal power wrapped in earthly gentleness. When faced with man's inhumanity to man—even in His own servants, as was the case when Peter and John demanded He call down fire from heaven and burn up some discourteous people who wouldn't give them hospitality—Jesus responded with meekness. He simply rebuked His men for their lack of understanding and compassion, reminded them the Son of Man had come to save men's lives and not destroy them—and moved on (Luke 9:52–56). This was not weakness, as some have supposed; rather, this heavenly meekness illustrates for us the power to control anger and respond with grace.

Paul the Apostle

When I think of Paul I think of meekness too—and this in the character of one of the strongest leaders of all. It was quite a surprise to discover how often Paul talked about gentleness. "As apostles of Christ we could have been a burden to you, but we were gentle among you, like a mother caring for her little children," he said to the Thessalonians (see 1 Thessalonians 2:7), while to Timothy he said, "The servant of the Lord must not strive; but be gentle unto all men, apt to teach, patient, In meekness instructing those that oppose themselves [those who oppose him he must gently instruct]" (2 Timothy 2: 24,25).

Now then, here we have it. We shall not be leaders very long before we have some servant oppose us. Whether it be a member of a committee we have been asked to head up, a baby-sitter who is abusing her privileges, or a staff member pushing us to the limit—it will happen! Then how will we respond?

Will strength and dignity be our clothing and the law of kindness be exercised, as we open our mouth with wisdom about the issue? Will we, as Moffatt's translation has it, talk "shrewd sense and offers kindly counsel" like a true Queen of Hearts? Or will we speak harshly, putting the offending party in his or her place, not bothering to explain the task or make the instructions clear?

Over and over again, Paul closed his letters with the words, "The grace of the Lord Jesus be with your spirit." I believe it is this gracious spirit, the very Spirit of the Christ manifest in the flesh two thousand years ago, we need to appropriate for ourselves, as we draw on His strength and dignity to deal with awkward people.

Moses

But then there was Moses. Now he gives me comfort. I never thought of Moses as gentle and meek. I thought of him as a huge, impatient man—huge in stature and huge in personality. I'm sure he was both. But I certainly never envisioned him as huge in humility and meekness. It came as a shock to me, therefore, to discover that God called him "very meek, above all the men who were upon the face of the earth" (Numbers 12:3). *Moses?* Well, surely God knew if he was meek or not. It came not only as a surprise, but also as a relief to read on in the man's story, and find out that every now and then he got sick of being meek. Now I could relate to that. He was humble but human—like me. His servant spirit slipped not a few times, as he was trying to cope with all these complaining, ornery people he was leading around the desert. Moses, of course, had always had a problem with his temper. That was the reason he ended up in the outreaches of the desert with a few scraggy sheep to look after. In the first place, he had lost his cool completely when he lived in

Egypt, and ended up killing one of Pharaoh's soldiers and hiding his body in the sand. This was known to Pharaoh, and fearing retribution, Moses fled to the wilderness. Forty years in that barren place helped somewhat to create a servant spirit in the man. After all, there's nothing like herding sheep in the desert hinterlands to keep you humble!

God, however, called him to go back and rescue his people from the hand of Pharaoh. Once or twice in the narrative, Moses flew into a rage, but in the end succeeded in his demands—with a little help from God (and the ten plagues) and off they all went to the Promised Land. The rest of the story is well known.

The Bible tells us Moses' prevailing attitude was one of meekness. The man was by and large the people's humble servant. He inspired a followship most of the time from most of the people. Did he *always* gently instruct those who opposed him? Was he *always* apt to teach? Did he habitually give a soft answer to the rabble who were amongst them when they caused constant trouble? Well, not always! He did break the tablets of the Ten Commandments on the ground at one point! (Of course, you always break the Ten Commandments when you lose control of your temper!) This, at least, showed some progress. A few years previously, he would have broken the tablets over the people's heads, so he was learning. Occasionally, he would rant and rave to God about the servant spirit he was expected to exhibit in the face of unbelievable provocation, as recorded for us in the Book of Numbers, Chapter 11:11–15, when he complained to God:

> Wherefore hast thou afflicted thy servant? and
> wherefore have I not found favour in thy
> sight, that thou layest the burden of all this
> people upon me? Have I conceived all this
> people? have I begotten them, that thou

shouldest say unto me, Carry them in thy
bosom, as a nursing father beareth the
sucking child, unto the land which thou
swarest unto their fathers? Whence should I
have flesh to give unto all this people? for
they weep unto me, saying, Give us flesh, that
we may eat. I am not able to bear all this
people alone, because it is too heavy for me.
And if thou deal thus with me, kill me, I pray
thee, out of hand, if I have found favour in
thy sight; and let me not see my
wretchedness.

The point I am trying to make is that—it all takes time!
Yes, many times Moses got sick of being meek, but he
worked at it—just as you and I have to do.

Time to Grow

Just as it takes time to grow a child, it takes time to grow
an attitude. The servant spirit springs from a growing
relationship with the Servant—the Lord's Servant who
dwells within us. As Christ's life fills us, old attitudes will
fall away.

When we used to minister to young people I would
always be impatient with the slow process of change in
the youngsters' lives. Many of them were wild, young
people with matching life-styles.

It took time, but I finally realized that our job was not
to spend time and energy pointing out the weaknesses of
the old life; our job was to stimulate and encourage the
new life within, so it would fill those teen-agers, and that
would take care of the problem. We needed to concentrate on the positives and watch the negatives fall away.
It takes *time* for that to happen.

So it is with a servant spirit. It takes time; time to learn how to let the new life of Jesus, God's Servant, invade every area of our being. There are rules to that process— rules we have to learn, to know, to do. If we get distracted, worrying obsessively about every time we blew it, we'll never get where we are going; or more accurately, let Him get where He is going! It takes a lifetime to become a servant of the Lord, and a servant of people.

Climb the Mountain

When Moses came down that Judean mountain after receiving the Law, and discovered his people drunk and naked, he totally lost control of himself. In the end, after meting out the punishment he deemed fit, he turned around to find his tablets of stone! There they were, smashed into smithereens. Those precious tablets containing the Ten Commandments, written by the finger of God, were broken beyond repair. Moses had to climb back up that tall mountain and start all over again! But climb it, he did. So each of us must do, until we get it right. Maturity doesn't grow all in a night.

When you think about the Queen of Hearts, serving as she did, you are thinking about a perfect model of a servant leader. You are also being given a picture of maturity. I get the idea this woman was getting to the point in her life when she was looking back on many more years than she was looking forward to. It had taken time for her to learn how to do all she was doing the way she was doing it. Perhaps, at the start of her marriage, she only had one servant. Now she had many. God takes us gently on in the lessons of leadership and servanthood, helping us take one step at a time.

Authority Is Accountable

One of the most helpful thoughts, as I consider servant leadership, has been the realization that however many people I have *under me,* I, myself, am under authority and am accountable. Even if I end up to be Queen of England (unlikely)—I will be accountable to Parliament! If I am to be a *woman that fears the Lord,* I well know I must give an account to Him of how I have exercised that leadership role.

Ephesians 6:7 tells me that "with good will doing service, as to the Lord, and not to men." This helps me to keep a servant spirit in mind as I lead.

If I am in authority, I also need to know this does not mean I am better than my servants. It is the position that is different, not the people in the positions. A true spirit of meekness tells me I am to esteem others better than myself, and not to think highly of myself. We are simply called to different functions in society and in the church, and I need to acknowledge the equality of my peers, yield to the authority of my superiors, and thoughtfully care for those for whom I am responsible—all in a spirit of meekness.

I need to *ask* people to do things for me rather than *tell* them to do them. There is a way of getting things done that does not leave the person who has been told to do the doing, feeling used. Those of us with strong personalities tend to be bossy. When I am truly bossed myself, it shows as I lead others.

A Bond Slave

Most helpful of all is to think about the words *bond servant* and just what that means.

In the New Testament the term means one who owed obligatory service to his master who had purchased and therefore owned him. Paul delighted in calling himself a bond slave of Jesus Christ. We have already talked about the personal freedom we can know when we count ourselves fully God's in this way, but I want to take three practical examples from the life of a slave to illustrate my point.

Time. First, a bond slave had no time of his own. Once sold to a master his time was his master's. He did not clock in or out. Neither did he clock-watch. He had no time that was his own, save that which his master designated.

So it is with the captured spirit of Christ's slave. *Time!* How precious a commodity that is to us, but once we belong to Christ, our time is His time. We have no time off other than He allows or suggests. This does not mean we can never go for a walk, play golf, or take a vacation. Jesus said to His disciples one day, "Come ye apart and rest awhile" (*see* Mark 6:31), but notice His disciples didn't tell Jesus when *they* decided to rest.

When I first became a Christian, this was probably the biggest tussle of my new life. Why, for eighteen years, I had decided exactly what to do with my free time! I would play tennis, date boys, go skating, buy clothes, rap with friends, party, or take a course in something that tickled my fancy. Then Christ came into my life and He began to send people who needed help my way. That took time— in the end, *all* of my time. But that was all right because I was living by God's clock, not mine. I learned that God's clocks keep perfect time—never fast, never slow, never stopping. I had to learn to live by that clock—by God's eternal calendar. I had to learn that from human time to human time God's heavenly alarm goes off and everlasting plans must supersede my human programming.

> *What is "man time" anyway? . . . God gave it,*
>   *created it for us.*
> *Dropped and suspended it in space, in the*
>   *middle of eternity,*
> *What makes it up anyhow?*
>   *Ordered moments*
>   *Packaged into minutes*

Growing to an hour
Slotting into months of days
Making tidy years go by.

As God has managed my time over the years, He has filled it with His tasks, and I have no regrets. *What would I have done with it?* I sometimes wonder. Certainly nothing as satisfying, as far-reaching as He has done with it!

I think of the Master's scheduling when my sick mother-in-law needed to be cared for in a period of my life that could only be described as hectic man time! And then there was the child in deep distress that appeared at my kitchen door, as I bathed my baby and watched two toddlers toddling into interminable trouble. I think of the homeless relative who needed a place to live and be encouraged; the group of women needing inspiration; the young married couple, looking for help with a flagging marriage. I think back and I remember how, as I have lived my life according to God's clock, not mine, there has always been time for people; and when that was the case, the lessons that I learned, the blessing and the growth in faith, were my grand reward. But most of all, there came to my heart at times like these, a quiet sense of precious eternal moments lent to me—for the here and now—God's great gift to me. "Only one life 'twill soon be past; only what's done for Christ will last."

Rights. Second, a slave had no rights. He was totally dependent upon his master for his very life. One of the privileges we hold most dear in this great country of ours is our *rights.* Our rights have become the predominant theme of our nation. The right to "life, liberty, and the pursuit of happiness" says it all. But a slave had no such rights. His very life belonged to his master; liberty was out of the question, save for the Israelites' slaves, when the year of Jubilee meant emancipation. And the very idea of the pursuit of happiness was ludicrous. A slave was a slave.

He had no rights—only wrongs. So it is with the Christian, the bond slave of Jesus Christ. Our very life belongs to our Master who may spend it anywhere and in any way He wishes. Sometimes a trusted slave might even be sent by his master on some dangerous assignment and spill his blood on foreign soil. Even a slave's wife and children belonged to his master. The strange part is that for the Christian, the whole of it is a matter of *voluntary servitude.* It is service born out of gratitude. Because we love our Master we "will not go out free" and only His rights matter to us. Our rights are then transformed into our responsibilities for God and for His Kingdom.

Pay. Third, there was the matter of money. A slave had no pay. Money was no problem to the slave for he acted simply as the good steward of his master's assets. His master may have given him money to trade with, or to pay other servants of lower rank, but it was always his master's money.

This has been the most difficult concept of all for me. My family was always extremely generous, and when Stuart and I went into full-time Christian work, we had very little money. I discovered what a bad steward I was. I had to learn the value of the stuff, but most importantly I had to remember none of it was mine! A slave had no money save that of his master's. This attitude surely makes you think twice before spending anything. Wouldn't *you* think twice before you spent someone else's money?

The captured servant knows he is captured! And with that concept, a new attitude toward his time, his rights, and his money is born.

Credit. Finally, the bond slave never took the credit for anything. All the credit belonged to his master. Since he was his master's property, all he achieved went to enhance his lord's reputation. One of the reasons we do not achieve very much for God is the need we have for recognition. We want to take the credit. We desperately need an audience; are consistently listening for applause; and long to soak in the accolades. There are too many Christians who refuse to serve the Lord without remuneration, insist on having their names on the program, and even demand interviews with the local press if they perform.

If we can only decide we are not going to worry *who* gets the credit, we will discover just how much Kingdom work gets done. We are often far too busy competing for prominence, producing a performance or protecting our turf to accomplish much.

A bond slave who did a good job handling his master's affairs would hear people honor his master because of it.

"What a fine master he must be to have had the wisdom to buy and train such an able slave," the people would say. The glory would be the master's.

A spiritual servant seeks to serve in such a way as to bring credit to the one served. Actually, a true servant wants to direct attention away from himself and focus the light on his master. Jesus Christ hardly ever opened His mouth without giving His Father the credit for the things He said and did.

"The Father that dwelleth in me, he doeth the works," He said (John 14:10.)

Summing Up

So, to sum up, the servant spirit is the Christlike spirit that begets service by example; rules meekly; esteems others better than himself; chooses team members carefully, regarding the position of authority as a trust. Once lent the place of leadership, however, a true servant leader carefully makes Christian choices, based on biblical principles with people, not profit, in mind. The servant spirit is also a controlled spirit, dressed in strength and dignity, talking shrewd sense, speaking the truth in love and offering kindly counsel along the way. What is more, the servant spirit is a captured spirit, chained by choice to the Lord and yoked to Him. He bears burdens for the Master that because of the slave's great love, feel strangely easy and light. The captured servant recognizes no rights at all, no time that is his own, no money that he can spend—nothing, in fact, that does not relate to his Master. That's all right. He knows he has been bought with a price—the price of the blood of his Master Himself, and therefore *all* the credit must go to Him.

When such a servant spirit rules and reigns within the heart of a woman, it will be almost certain that she will find herself at the end of her day—queen of her servants' hearts!

WORKSHEET

Read these points to ponder from chapter 4 and spend five minutes doing so.

- The Queen of Hearts was a perfect model of a servant leader.
- She exhibited a sweet servant spirit even very early in the morning.
- Do you have a servant spirit or a snappy spirit?
- Are you able to see a raw gift in someone? To discern where a person's capabilities lie?
- Capabilities are nice, of course, and a caring attitude essential, but a good dose of common sense makes up for a lot.
- We do not have a crisis of leadership so much as a crisis of followship.
- The Queen of Hearts was a capable woman who was a born leader, knowing how to be strong in a dignified way—forceful but feminine.
- Domination isn't leadership.
- Meekness is controlled strength.

- I need to ask people to do things for me, rather than tell them to do them. There is a way of getting things done that does not leave the person who has been told to do the doing, feeling used.

- A slave had no time, no rights, no pay, and always gave the credit to his master.

- If we can only decide we are not going to worry who gets the credit, we will discover just how much Kingdom work gets done!

1. **What Do They Say?**
   a) What does Jesus say about being a servant leader? Read the following verses and discuss: John 13:2–17
   b) What does Paul say? 1 Corinthians 4:1–5; Romans 12:10,11; Galatians 6:1
   c) What does Peter say? 1 Peter 2:21; 5:2–5

2. **What Does She Do?**
   What do you learn about servant leadership from the Queen of Hearts?

3. **Let's Pretend.**
   Pretend you are a bond slave. Which of the following words would give you most problems and why?
   > *no time*
   > *no rights*
   > *no pay*
   > *no credit*

4. **Prayer Time**
   Are you queen of your servants' hearts? Pray about it.

CHAPTER
5

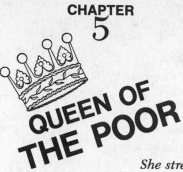

QUEEN OF THE POOR

*She stretcheth her hand
to the poor; yea, she reacheth forth
her hands to the needy.*

Verse 20

THERE SEEMS TO BE NOTHING OUR QUEEN OF HEARTS does not do! Here she is reaching outside her circle of rich acquaintances to help the poor and needy. Helping hands! But then your hands don't do anything on their own. Hands do what the heart instructs them to do. Hands do the practical things that spring from the principles that we believe. The Queen of Hearts knows she is blessed to be a blessing, and uses "the fruit of her hands" to bless the poor. She "labors working with her hands the thing which is good, that she may have to give to him that needeth" (*see* Ephesians 4:28). She works that she may *have to give*—not have to have or have to have *more.* Her hands hold the distaff or the mending instrument. She is frugal with her housekeeping, and she is never idle. All this, that she may reach out her hands to meet other people's needs.

Who Are the Poor?

I asked a Salvation Army officer that question. He answered me quickly and surely. "Those who are unable to care for themselves because they lack the basic necessities of life." "Then, what are the basic necessities?" I inquired. "Food, shelter, clothing, and work—the means of providing those things," he replied.

Who are the poor? The poor are the majority of the two hundred thousand people that will be born today in the Third and Fourth Worlds. These are the have-not people who are multiplying with terrifying rapidity. The population explosion means that 1 billion people will go to bed hungry tonight, and fifteen thousand will not wake up tomorrow morning.

I was accumulating the facts and figures for this chapter during a recent flight, and I noticed a smartly dressed young business executive type watching me with interest. I shared some of my findings with him, whereupon he simply shrugged his shoulders and commented, "If I saw those people in those countries doing an honest day's work, I'd feel like they deserved helping!" His comment was all too common and showed a total ignorance of the helplessness of millions of people who would love to do an honest day's work—*if it was there to do!* I asked him *if* work did happen to be available, as was the case in some places, did he think he could do a good job on a diet of one-half cup of rice a day? I wondered if his children could learn to better themselves in schools (where there were such luxuries), when they had suffered brain damage through malnutrition? So many of the Third and Fourth World (developing and least developed) countries have such few natural resources, technical abilities, or health facilities, it means that extreme poverty reigns supreme, and people simply are incapable of helping themselves.

The Eternal Compulsory Fast

Who are the poor? The people who have little or nothing to eat and therefore cannot work, or do not have work, so they cannot eat. The vicious cycle has no end. Over one-half of the entire world is chronically hungry. In India, one-quarter million people live on the city sidewalks, reduced to foraging for food in the garbage dumps like dogs. World Concern says, "For one-half to two-thirds of the people alive on our planet today, hunger is not merely an acute pang felt before lunch—it's a life-style!" Mahatma Gandhi called these people's plight "The Eternal Compulsory Fast."

Living Water

Then there is the problem of water. We cannot live ten days without this commodity, and yet just to have it around isn't the answer either. For instance, what *sort* of water is available for people in the developing nations? Often the water is contaminated, infested with parasites and waste products. You may as well wash with mud. In some areas of the world, the same water is used for washing, drinking, and bathing!

Disease

When there is only one doctor around to look after 61,800 folk (as in Africa's Upper Volta), common disease becomes fatal. How can a single doctor care for so many people, with primitive medicine? He can only be as effective as a painter painting over rust! Before long the rust devours.

Then there are uncommon diseases like river blindness. First, the black fly injects its larvae under the skin of its victim. Then the larvae hatch and develop into foot-long spaghettilike worms that literally swim under the skin, permeate the tissues throughout the body, making for their prime target—the cornea. Once there, they feast their fill with the result that 30 million people in those places go blind by the age of 40. In some areas, 40 percent of all adults are blind! The nightmare proportions of this ghastly reality are such that few doctors are lining up to establish their practices in these regions. Anyway their medicine would be useless, even if they did, for there is absolutely no cure for this disease. And this is just one of the diseases that are busy snatching people away into eternity.

Strangers

Then there are those who are not dressed up with nowhere to go. The refugees who roam our world greet us most days of the week, confronting our consciences from the covers of *Time* or *Newsweek*. *Life* magazine graphically portrays their living deaths for us, and if you visit Hong Kong, you can go and see for yourself the postage-stamp rooms, where forty people live in an area the size of a king-size bed. Some of us struggle with our relationships when we are living with two or three other people under the same roof. How would we manage, I wonder, sharing our living room with ten families or more? So who are the poor? They are destitute people who cannot, for all these reasons and more, care for or better themselves.

Why Are the Poor?

"Is there not then enough food to go around? Not enough grain in our big wide world for all these poor hungry people?" As we travel through the farmlands of Wisconsin and see the seas of golden grain or pick and choose from our richly stacked supermarket shelves, it's almost impossible to believe one-half the world is eternally hungry. Isn't there really enough food to go around?

Oh, yes, there is, and that's the shocking part. There is easily enough food to feed the entire world. The problem is it is so unequally distributed. Listen to some stark facts for a moment.

Less than 6 percent of the West's population live in the USA. We demand three-fourths of the world's protein every year and consume double what we need. We get this protein mainly from meat, and the shocking fact is that 40 percent of the USA population is overweight. One-half the deaths in our nation are attributed to factors connected with overeating. How is it we are eating ourselves to death, while others in our globe village are starving to death? Ronald J. Sider, in his book *Rich Christians in an Age of Hunger* (Inter-Varsity, 1977) tells us that a 1970 U.N. estimate says we need only to find 12 million added tons of grain to be able to feed 460 million malnourished people. That is only 30 percent of what we feed our cattle—the cattle we are getting fat eating! "Well, that was in 1970," you counter. Correct. And it's more than a decade worse now!

Energy

Then there is our consuming passion for energy. In our country, according to Sider, "air conditioning alone uses as much energy per year as does the entire country of China *annually* with its 830 million people." This is an extremely serious situation. A scientist, speaking on TV concerning the energy crisis, made this comment, "If we continue to insist on the kind of energy-consuming life we've been used to—we'll have to fight a war for it!" "Well, now, that's okay if we do," some die-hard people answer. "We're ready to fight a war if it's necessary to control our assets, to enjoy our luxuries, to keep our hoarded resources intact. We will fend off anyone who dares to reach out his hand to threaten our way of life. Anyway," they usually add proudly, "our government gives more than anyone in the world for the hungry!" (Arthur Simon, *Bread for the World*). Wrong again! That is a myth. We are not very generous at all, where giving to world hunger is concerned. In fact, we are fifth from the bottom of a list of seventeen countries seeking to help. That's right—fifth from the bottom! The USA is number thirteen out of seventeen countries in percentage of Gross National Product given among the major Western donors of foreign aid!

Hoarding

Hoarding is very shortsighted. Apart from the indirect Christian teaching concerning giving to the poor, the worsening world hunger seriously threatens all possibilities for world peace. "There are more hungry people today than ever before, and failure to satisfy their needs could have grave implications for us all," Warren Brown of the *Washington Post* warns. Quite so—with special emphasis on the *grave!* What if the have-nots rise up, figuring it's better to die, fighting for a scrap of food, than to die the slow death of starvation? What about the Third and Fourth World countries that either have or will shortly have their own nuclear devices? What about nuclear blackmail?

There is such a thing as "lifeboat ethics." This philosophy is being taught by such eminent people as Dr. Garrett Hardin, a prominent biologist. It is unfortunately a philosophy accepted by huge numbers of people. It goes like this: "We should not help the poor countries with food or aid. Each rich country is a lifeboat that will survive only if it refuses to waste its very limited resources on the hungry masses swimming in the water around it . . . since poor countries "irresponsibly" permit unrestrained population growth, starvation is the only way to check the ever-growing number of hungry mouths. Hence, increased aid merely postpones the day of reckoning. When it comes, our aid will only have preserved even more persons for ultimate starvation. Therefore it is ethically correct to help them learn the hard way—by letting them starve now!" *(Rich Christians in an Age of Hunger).* The queen of the Lord's heart rejects such a philosophy out of hand, knowing her Lord considered and cared for the poor. She reaches out her hands to the waterlogged wretches swimming in the waters around her boat. She stretches her resources to meet their desperate need, and for this reason the queen of the Lord's heart is queen of the poor.

Excuses—Bureaucracy

Of course, to be fair it's idealistic to imagine it is a simple act to meet the needs of the poor. The people who put forward a lifeboat ethic often point out (and sadly, quite rightly) that there is a lot of incompetency among the agencies that handle charity funds and relief supplies for poor people.

Bias

Then there is the problem of the ambivalence of the church. Many churches have moved from downtown areas, away from city centers, out of sight of deteriorating neighborhoods. The people that now worship in the middle-class neighborhoods are not so graphically reminded of the inner-city needs anymore. In the past, it has generally been the so-called liberal churches that have done the "social work" and many evangelical communities have felt the Gospel has been lost in the "service" side of activity.

Basically the problem lies in a biblical illiteracy. A Christian attitude to the poor must grow out of an understanding of God's concern for human suffering. We must get ourselves a Bible, a notebook, and a few hours quiet time. Ask God to help us develop a biblical view of the poor.

If we are not full of God's thoughts on the matter, we

will be influenced by worldly thinking and open to any-one's theories! When you ask me, "Why should I care?" I have to tell you, you have to care because Jesus did, and Jesus said that we must if we would please Him. If I would be queen of His heart, I must be queen to the poor. My mind must be acquainted with the frightening facts and my heart touched by them. Sider asks, "Dare we let a child die in someone's arms tonight for the lack of a cup of powdered milk or a spoonful of rice? When we repre-sent the wealth of North America, and especially Bible-believing America, where even a fraction of that wealth could save millions of children from starvation, in a world where the rich minority feed more grain to their livestock than all the people in India or China eat, it is absurd and immoral to talk of the necessity of letting selected hungry nations starve to death" (*Rich Christians in an Age of Hunger*).

Where Are the Poor?

Be assured, the poor are within reach. They are within reach of my prayers and concern, my pocketbook, and my energy. But it will mean a stretching and growing to ac-commodate the personal concern that the hand requires. Someone asked a young missionary candidate what it was going to take to alleviate the world's needs. "Bent knees, wet eyes and a broken heart," was the answer. *That's* what it's going to take.

The poor must have a permanent place in the warp and woof of my thinking, planning, and actions. I am re-minded of this in Isaiah 58:6,7 when Jehovah tells Israel, in effect: "This is what I require of you. Loose the fetters of injustice, untie the knots of the yoke, snap every yoke and set free those that are crushed. Share your food with the hungry, take the homeless poor into your home. Clothe the naked when you meet them and never evade a duty to your kinfolk" (*see* NEB).

The challenge to Israel in the past comes to us now in the present. We must become personally responsible to find out *where* the poor are that we can reach, and then get on with it.

A Biblical Perspective

For Christians the power of sin and selfishness has been broken. We belong, if we have been born from above, to One who creates within us an entirely new set of personal, social, and economic standards. As we begin to read the Word of God, we discover biblical models that God created in Old Testament times. He put into process mechanisms and structures to prevent great economic inequality among His people. God very definitely is seen as a God that disapproved of extremes of wealth.

It all began in the agrarian society of Old Testament times, when the land was used as capital—the basic means of producing wealth. God came up with a plan that was totally radical! This plan reminded Israel of a vital basic principle. We are only stewards, and God demands economic justice from those that profess to belong to Him.

Jubilee Principle

You can read all about God's radical reasons for instructing Moses to put His plan into operation in Leviticus 25:10–24. "The land shall not be sold for ever: for the land is mine . . ." says the Lord in verse 23. The theological basis for the Jubilee idea was that Yahweh owned the land. Private property could be kept, but every fifty years, all land was to return to the original owners—without compensation. The means of producing wealth was to be equalized regularly. The poor had the right to receive back land at the time of Jubilee, and therefore be enabled to help themselves—to have a way of making their own way again—their own living.

"The poor have rights," God explained, "and don't you forget it!" This way they have the chance to dignity—the chance to work and provide for their families' basic needs.

The Sabbatical Year

Every seventh year in Old Testament times, the slaves were to be liberated, and the soil left fallow. The proceeds of the resting ground were to belong to the poor. As the ground was left alone during that seventh year, it still produced. It was then up to the poor to harvest its fruits and store them up for the lean years. "That the poor of your people may eat," explained Jehovah. Jehovah was not—and is not—content to see one-half of His world chronically hungry. He tried to show the world the way He felt by giving Israel these and other laws that would model another way to cruel unbelieving nations around them, and that the poor were not to be ground into the dust! If Israel would but obey the laws given by Jehovah, they were told there would be "no poor in Israel" (*see* Deuteronomy 15:4) but unfortunately they didn't obey them, and the poor remained poor, bringing the wrath and punishment of God upon the Jewish nation.

Tithing and Gleaning

The law made provisions for one-tenth of the farm produce to be given to the poor, the fatherless, the widows, and sojourners (foreigners): "That the Lord your God may bless you!" This—because God is God of the poor. The leaders of the nation were soberly warned of the consequences of reneging on their responsibilities. Those in authority were expected to give a good example in this regard. King Lemuel remembered his mother's wise advice on the subject and wrote it down, "Open your mouth and judge righteously the rights of the afflicted and the needy!" (*see* verse 9). He was exhorted to avoid strong drink lest he "forgot what is decreed and pervert the rights of the afflicted" (*see* verse 5). The ancient law of tithing remembered those rights and sought to redress them.

Now I am not purporting to say we need to return California to the Mexicans, and the rest of America to the Indians, and let the poor of Milwaukee go and milk a farmer's cow every seventh year. But the basic principles of all these things apply today. We need to think of creative ways of putting caring concerns into some concrete form to fit our own age, even as the children of Israel were instructed to do in theirs.

A Common Life of Mutual Availability

When we get to the New Testament, we learn that there is to be a loving oneness among Christians—one that is to be so visible that it convinces the world that Christ came from the Father (John 17:20–23). We have our example given to us by the Lord Jesus Himself in the Gospels. Jesus and the poor were inseparable. The needy flocked around Him everywhere He went. The beggars, the blind, the lame, the destitute, with no other place to go. The hungry, too—and He was touched by all of them. Many times we read that Jesus was moved with compassion for the multitude who were as "sheep without the shepherd." One time when Jesus had had some bad news about the death of John the Baptist, his cousin and friend, He told the disciples to get into a boat and go across the lake that they might have some time to recover, recoup, and pray. When they got there, the crowd had anticipated their movements and had swarmed around the lake, arriving tired and hungry but eager to hear Jesus' Word and see His wonderful miracles. Jesus was touched; convulsed with compassion, and putting His own personal sorrows aside, He attended to their needs (Matthew 14:13,14).

Interrupted by the Multitude

When Jesus was interrupted by a multitude of need, He mended it, at considerable cost to Himself. When we are interrupted by such unwelcome intrusions, we tend to react as the disciples did saying, "Send them away that they may go into the villages and buy themselves food!" Notice Jesus' answer, "They need not depart; give ye them to eat." (*See* verses 15–21.) They *need not* depart you know! "But," you protest as Philip did, "two hundred dollars (or two thousand dollars) worth of food isn't sufficient for them that everyone might take a little!" The size of the world's hungry mouth often stops us from even trying to feed it the small morsel we might be able to give. But we have forgotten something. In His hands the little we have is multiplied. We give what we have, not what we have not. A little lad, seeing the situation, was willing to go hungry and placed his inadequate lunch into the hands of God. Jesus could have his lunch—that was fine by him. The Son of God must have smiled at the boy who was obviously poor himself, since barley loaves were the fare of poor folk. But then the poor are marvelously generous to their own kind, and Jesus must have been happy about that too.

Anyway, the disciples learned a very important lesson. *A little is enough.* The important thing is that the little lad *reached* with his little lunch. He reached out his hands to the poor with barley loaves and two small fish, and gave what he had. By the time Jesus had finished blessing his gift, five thousand people had been fed. What's more, each of the twelve apostles had a whole basketful of bread for themselves! Now, then, if only we could get the principles straight in our heads. Jesus cares for the poor. He wants His disciples to care, too. He wants His disciples to pool their inadequate resources and reach out their hands to the poor to give what they have—not what they have not. He longs to see His disciples get organized; to break the multitude of need down to manageable groups of people, and start just where they are, *doing* what they can —not what they cannot!

Jesus stretched the disciples' comprehension that day. He showed them He was on the side of the poor and insisted that they "need not depart" when *they*, His disciples, could draw on Him to help feed them.

Jesus told us in a most memorable passage of Scripture that He takes it personally when we feed the hungry, visit the prisoner, or clothe the naked. ". . . Inasmuch as ye have done it unto one of the least of these my brethren, ye have done it unto me," He said in Matthew 25:40.

In the same breath, He added, ". . . Inasmuch as ye did it not to one of the least of these, ye did it not to me" (verse 45).

The Common Caring

The Acts of the Apostles tells of a company of common people who were completely available to each other. In fact, in Acts 4:32 we have these astonishing words, "No one said that any of the things which he possessed were his own, but they had everything in common." The early Church practiced a pattern of economic sharing. They regularly dipped into their capital reserves to help the poor. Barnabas sold a field, and not only this generous man but "as many as were possessors of lands or houses sold them . . . and distribution was made unto every man according as he had need" (*see* Acts 4:34,35).

"The early church did not insist on absolute economic equality. Nor did they abolish private property. . . . Sharing was voluntary, not compulsory" (as Peter reminded Ananias, Acts 5:4). That did not mean that everyone donated everything. "In fact, the tense of Acts 3:45 and 4:34 infers 'They *often* sold possessions . . . or they were in the habit of bringing the proceeds of what was being sold' " (Sider).

These people gave until needs were met. As they saw a problem, they dealt with it. What a huge challenge this is to us all!

This means that I need to hold all of my goods in trust. It is not *my* house I keep clean, *my* car I fill with gas, *my* fridge I pack with food, but *His*. I am part of His Body the Church, and if I see a member of His Body in need I must meet it out of *my* wealth.

"But I'm not wealthy," you object. "If I was, I would give." God sees what we give in relation to what we have, not in relation to what we have not! He also sees what we keep! The widow's mite was worth millions as far as Jesus was concerned, while the mercenary Pharisees gave meager mites in the Saviour's eyes!

Ken

Years ago when Stuart and I were working in England we were just about making ends meet—and that only with a lot of tugging at both ends! I had seen a special boy find Christ and grow rapidly in the Lord. One day he came to me and asked what I thought about the idea of his going to Bible School. I thought it was a great idea. There was a problem however: Ken had no funds. He supported his mother and helped with his younger brothers' financial concerns. The youth group of which he was a part was made aware of the problem. One girl began to work overtime "laboring with her hands that which was good that she might have to give"—to Ken. Another gave up the money he used to see his favorite soccer team play.

Others sold precious items and gave to the "common cause."

And what did I do? Well, I was faced with a real dilemma. At that time I literally had no extra cash.

One night a friend came down to my house in order for me to cut her hair. To my amazement she gave me a thank you note with ten pounds inside. As soon as she gave it to me I knew it was for Ken. The next day as I scribbled him a little note, I opened our mail. Inside was a bill for ten pounds! Now I was in a quandary. Apart from the money my friend had given me, I had absolutely no funds to pay that bill!

Eventually I put the ten pounds in Ken's card and posted it and then returned home to go through my closets and search for something to sell. That very afternoon as I was foraging through my cupboards, a neighbor stopped by and told me she loved the way I had fixed my friend's hair, and asked me if I would fix hers and her kids' for ten pounds! And so I labored, working with my hands that which was good that I may have to give. What joy! It isn't a question of giving only if I am so rich it won't hurt. It is a question of getting my head on straight, biblically, and realizing nothing I have is my own. I merely hold it in trust for my God and my sisters and brothers in Christ.

Where Do I Begin?

So very practically—what can *I* do to help? Where do *I* start? Who do *I* talk to?

First of all we need to get informed. Here are some of the most practical ways I can think of of doing that! Take a periodical or magazine telling you the facts. World Vision, World Concern, or World Relief have publications that are an excellent help. Read a book or two on the subject. I would suggest *Rich Christians in an Age of Hunger* by Ronald J. Sider, *Moved with Compassion* by

Eva den Hartog, and *World of Hope in the Midst of Despair* by Henry Maule. Visit your nearest Salvation Army headquarters and see what they are doing. Be around late at night when the homeless are brought to the shelter. Find out if anything is being done in the local jail. Write to Charles Colson Prison Fellowship Ministries to inquire how *you* can get involved. Call the government agency dealing with food distribution for the unemployed in your town and start a food pantry at your church. Find out how many refugees there are in your area and organize a loving group to welcome and minister to them. We did this to great effect in our Elmbrook Church and now serve eight hundred refugees. Decide which agency shall have your regular monetary donations. (Be sure it is an organization that puts your money to good use and makes certain it reaches its target.) Take a vacation in Africa or South America instead of West Palm Beach or Hawaii. Visit some missionaries in poor places. Go to India or the Sub-Sahara regions of the world—you'll never be the same again! Make sure your children are well informed as well, and instruct them in these matters, even as Lemuel's mother instructed him. Short term missionary service will open a teen-ager's eyes to the poor and their needs as nothing else will and they will come back rich in faith and love! (See end of this chapter for addresses for these suggestions.)

Try to interest the youth pastor of your fellowship to take a work party to a needy area, *as well as organizing kids' camps this summer.* (Notice I didn't say *instead of* organizing camps—I said *as well as!*)

The Gift of Citizenship

Someone has said, "Citizenship in a democracy is a gift that U. S. Christians often overlook." Discuss with your friends the opportunities that we have to influence public-policy decisions that affect people in need. Can you see ways that we can be ministers and advocates for the poor (and therefore for Jesus Himself), as we participate in the political process? Paul Simon, a U. S. Representative from Illinois noted, "Someone who sits down and writes a letter about hunger . . . almost literally has to be saving a life. . . ." Write that letter today! In some or all of these ways, you can begin to care for the poor.

So reach out your hands, stretch a little; grow up straight and tall before the Lord; please His heart by considering the poor and laboring with your hands, that the fruit of your labors might help to meet their needs.

And do all this for the sake of the One who "though he was rich . . . became poor, that [we] through his poverty might be rich" (2 Corinthians 8:9).

Reaching

The Queen of Hearts started where she was with what she had. She was aware of her neighborhood and the troubled people that lived there. First, we need to reach out just where *we* are. It is an incredible thing to me that we can live such isolated lives, not even knowing the name of folks who live next door, in the name of respecting their privacy and independence. "It's none of my business," we say shrugging our shoulders when we are told our neighbor has lost his job. God has made it *His* business to care, and what is His business is your business and my business. There may be real financial and material need right next door that we can tactfully alleviate.

One Christian I know heard the rumor that the husband of a young girl who lived on his street had just run out on her. "That's their concern, not mine," said the man. "I have enough trouble keeping my own marriage intact without worrying about anybody else's!" Little did he know that within three months, the young mother, not knowing what to do, had allowed herself to get into such a financial mess that she was selling her blood to the blood bank to help put food on the table! Start by looking at the need within reach; then reach out and reach it.

Stretching

Reaching leads to stretching. Getting involved expands you as a person. "I could *never* go to Asia as a missionary," expostulated a single woman. "But couldn't you help us find eating utensils and blankets for a refugee family from Laos that will be coming to Milwaukee tonight?" she was asked. "Sure I can do *that,*" she responded. Guess what happened. Starting where she was, she reached out and touched a need. And those needy Asian people reached right back and touched *her.* Two years later she is being stretched beyond her wildest dreams, as she proposes to go to Hong Kong with a relief organization! It's a pretty stretching thing to fill needs—real needs. You discover a God-given capacity for caring concern that leads to loving action you would not have believed you were capable of.

Little Ones to Him Belong

Teaching in Liverpool, I couldn't help but be made aware of poor people's problems. Some of the little guys (five and six year olds) would come to school at 8 A.M., struggling to keep their eyes open. I discovered they had been up till midnight, waiting outside the pub till dad had finished his drinking, so they could go home. One of these children took my heart in his hands and squeezed it into a question mark! I suddenly had to find out *why* he was so washed out and quiet and miserable—and all too often sported a bright-purple bruise on the side of his little face.

So one day I took his hand and told him I was going to walk him home. I found an unbelievable hovel of a house.

I knew I would never be the same again if I simply left my small charge behind and went home to my beautiful, clean home; and yet at the same time I also knew I would never be the same again if I tried to do something about it!

I decided to stretch! But what could I do? Where could I start? I prayed, "God, You are the God of the poor; I am Your Queen of Hearts. Show me what to do and I'll do it." "Where's Mother," I asked the little boy. "She caught on fire," he answered casually! "She's in 'ospital. She was smokin' and drunk too much and a rag got on fire." "That's where you start, my girl," I said to myself, and off we went to meet mother. She told me the government was going to help get them a better place to live, but they were low on the list and it could be months before anything was done. Then I met Dad, an older brother, and an older sister.

Who could care about such people, I wondered? *Only* God could really love them. God was going to have to stretch my capacity and make love happen in my heart— and He did! He just needed permission.

Stretching Makes You a Bigger Person

So we have to start out by reaching what we can reach and touching what we can touch. Then look out. The choice will come! "Will you be stretched?" God will ask, and we will have to answer that question.

A *yes* may take us to the uttermost parts of the earth, or it may involve us in the great need on our doorstep— only God knows where it will all end up—but the choice is ours. Let me quote J. Sidlow Baxler: "When the choice comes, Intellect says—I couldn't do anything wiser, Conscience says—I couldn't do anything better, Reason says —I couldn't do anything saner—but the Will says No!"

That is, if you are not a Queen of Hearts! If you are, of course, your world of the poor stands a chance of being a little bit different because He changed *you*—and you cared!

WORKSHEET

Read these points to ponder from chapter 5 and spend five minutes doing so.

- "For one-half to two-thirds of the people alive on our planet today, hunger is not merely an acute pang felt before lunch —it's a life-style!" Mahatma Gandhi called these people's plight "The Eternal Compulsory Fast."

- If you visit Hong Kong you can go and see for yourself the postage-stamp rooms where forty people live in an area the size of a king-size bed.

- There is easily enough food to feed the entire world. The problem is it is so unequally distributed.

- Lifeboat ethics says, "Our aid will only have preserved even more persons for ultimate starvation—therefore it is ethically correct to help them learn the hard way—by letting them starve now."

- Be assured the poor are within reach.

- When Jesus was interrupted by a multitude of need, He mended it, at considerable cost to Himself.

- We give what we have—not what we have not.

- Start by looking at the need within reach; then reach out and reach it!

- Reaching and stretching always makes you a bigger person.

- When the choice comes, Intellect says—I couldn't do anything wiser, Conscience says—I couldn't do anything better, Reason says—I couldn't do anything saner—but the Will says No! That is, if you are not a Queen of Hearts!

1. **How Much Do You Know About the Poor?**
   a) Discuss:
   Who are the poor?
   Where are the poor?
   Why are the poor?
   b) What does the Old Testament say about the poor?
   What does Jesus say? Matthew 25:35-46
   c) Discuss the Jerusalem model. Acts 4:34,35

2. **As Christians—**
   a) How do we get informed?
   b) How can we get involved?

3. **Sharing**
   Share a personal experience of stretching out your hands to the needy.

4. **Prayer Time**
   a) Consider the poor—silently for five minutes
   b) Pray for the poor—corporate prayer

Where to Reach Out

World Relief Fund
450 Gundersen
P. O. Box WRC
Wheaton, IL 60187

World Vision
919 W. Huntington Dr.
Monrovia, CA 91016

Prison Fellowship
P. O. Box 40562
Washington, DC 20016

Teen Missions International, Inc.
P. O. Box 1056
Merritt Island, FL 32952

World Concern
Box 33000
Seattle, Washington 98133

Pastor Dick Robinson
Elmbrook Church
777 S. Barker Road
Waukesha, WI 53186

QUEEN OF THE MERCHANTS' HEARTS

*She is like the
merchants' ships; she bringeth her food
from afar. . . . She perceiveth that her
merchandise is good. . . .*

Verses 14,18

Latchkey Kids

OURS IS THE GENERATION OF THE LATCHKEY KIDS.
Sixty percent of mothers with children under eighteen
years of age are currently working all day. Fifty percent
of these women are mothers, with preschoolers. There is
no grandma in sight either—she's working too! Sexual
roles are changing. We don't think in old-fashioned
terms of a mommy and a daddy and a couple of kids
anymore. The concept of family has become almost a
quaint anachronism.

That is not to say two grown-up people are not featured
in a little child's life nowadays, but they are not necessarily two people of the opposite sex. Often two women—
Mom and the baby-sitter—care for the toddler. As I talk
to women, I find no lack of caring concern for the little
ones, but there certainly seems to be a huge struggle with
conscience. Mother is wondering, *What am I doing to my
child, to my relationship with my husband, to myself and
to my God? If I have a choice about the matter, should I*

be working at all? Those women who economically have no choice wrestle with disturbing guilt as to what long-term effects their absence from home will have upon their children.

The Christian woman faces an added dilemma. Traditionally, the submissive wife has been protected from the world behind the barricade of her husband's authority and the walls of her home. She wonders what Scripture has to say about her coming over the top, and emerging triumphantly in the job market, capturing many of the man's opportunities, and climbing the corporate ladder. Here in Proverbs 31 we find the model of a godly working woman, and that from a passage of Scripture used in the past to point out the traditional domestic duties of the docile spouse. Our Queen of Hearts was a working woman, seemingly, coping with many of the challenges of our modern-day world. She had no mechanical helps around as we have, and yet she managed to do it all, and finish up with children that adored her, a husband who praised her, servants that obeyed her, and traders that appreciated her. Yes, she was even queen of the merchants' hearts!

Image

One of the questions a committed Christian woman has to ask herself is "What happens to my image if I return to work?" We should be concerned about that, as God made both male and female, and made them different. "Will I lose my femininity if I launch out into a career of my own?" We need to ask ourselves this.

If we have nothing to do on a rainy afternoon, we can go to the library, pick up a history book, and read about the Amazons. The warriors of this warlike tribe were women. The women cut off one of their breasts in order to pull the bow strings tighter. In other words, they sold their femininity in pursuit of their goals. "But I don't want to be an Amazonlike woman," I hear you say! Why even the Queen of Hearts sounds a little Amazonish to me. Doesn't it say, "She girdeth her loins with strength, and strengtheneth her arms" (verse 17)? And then again "She is like the merchants' ships . . ."(verse 14). Well, I must agree she does sound a bit like the *Titanic,* and yet the image of the modern woman, though a strong one, is not necessarily *un*feminine. Even *Time* magazine has featured a beautiful Amazonlike girl on its cover: COMING ON STRONG: THE NEW IDEAL OF BEAUTY the headline declared. The article informed us that this new ideal woman has a body made for motion, "for long, purposeful strides across the backcourt, through the mall, into the boardroom. It is a body that speaks assurance in itself and in the woman who, through will power and muscle power, has created it. In the old days, when women's shapes were expected to be either pillows or posts, today's muscular women might have been considered a freak. No more" (*Time* magazine, August 30, 1982). High energy living is here to stay, and with it, a new image for the working women, a new body, new clothes, new nutrition, and a new job to match. It is a new world of work that we see women stooping to conquer, and it's a male world at that, that they are exhorted to take by storm.

Our Queen of Hearts certainly found her world to be a male-dominated place. She sold real estate, was in the wine business, and got involved in planting her vineyard with the money she made from her most profitable ventures. She was a woman who worked hard both in her home and out of it.

Homemakers Work Too!

Let me say at this point, women who choose to stay at home *work!* Is there ever an end to it? There's a difference between homemaking and housekeeping, and it takes a Queen of Hearts to make a home out of a house and keep it that way. Sometimes when I chat to women who have chosen to stay at home, they sound very defensive, as if they are an endangered species and have to justify their position. "I work just as hard in the home as my friends do out of it," they tell me earnestly. A young mother complained to me not long ago, "Some of my friends who work make me feel as if I'm sloughing off." "What do you mean *sloughing off?*" I replied. "Why, I remember when I had three little ones under school age as you do, I worked harder than I ever had in the whole of my life!" Having worked out of the home most of our twenty-five years of marriage, I would have to say that for me, homemaking has been by far the greatest challenge of all.

After all, who prepares you for it? The hours are terrible —and if you have babies there's a night shift thrown in! The pay is minimal (if any), and promotion is unheard of. More often than not, even vacations mean everyone has a marvelous time, except mother, who finds herself working harder than she does at home, cooking over campfires, washing the children's clothes without adequate facilities, and trying to play policeman to the thousands of cousins, nephews, and friends that seem to appear out of the blue at such times.

No wonder women want to return to the working world for a rest!

If we are looking for an escape from the mundane syndrome at home (and the seemingly endless and unfair demands we may encounter there), then work outside those boundaries offers a tempting alternative. But I believe that is the worst possible motivation for returning to work. *Escape is no answer.*

Actually, you need to make absolutely sure you have a good handle on things at home *before* you ever contemplate taking on another job outside of it. It is true that extra money can pay for house help, *but* if you don't know how to help the house help, that's not going to help the house! And anyway, a Christian mother's first priority has to be her family and her home—all other work being supplementary and complementary.

Get Organized

The Queen of Hearts rose up a great while before day and organized her help (verse 15). Actually the Bible says, she cooked their breakfast for them. She had mastered the skill of homemaking *before* she ever set out to master her skills in the marketplace. She had hired help, but she didn't abdicate her responsibility. She knew exactly what needed to be done, how it needed to be done, and when it needed to be done, and her maidens were left in no doubt as to their duties, and just what it was she expected of them.

Whether we like housework or not we have to master it, or it will master us, no *matter how much help we have!* I learned that I needed to learn some expertise at home before I could ever properly delegate that work to someone else.

The Art of Leaving Things Undone

Stuart has been a great help in this area, being very flexible and patient, and I especially appreciate this, when I remember he had a mother whom I *swear* polished the pebbles on the path, and I suspect stood around the house with a dustpan in her hand, waiting for the particles of dust to alight! Whenever I have been working, and there has been too much to handle, Stuart has always helped me rearrange my scheduling. Sometimes he has helped me with the jobs, so that the house was never just a *house,* but always a home—comfortable, pretty, and kept moderately clean and tidy. I used the word *moderately* because that's the way it is if you take on a job outside the home when the family is still inside! Some things have to be left undone. Some things have to wait. Perhaps the wisdom to know what must be left undone is one of the secrets of juggling roles. Unless a balance can be struck that is acceptable to the family as a whole, a messy house can be the start of messy relationships between dads and moms, or parents and children.

Once the decision is finally made for mother to return to work, however, there is still the question of *image*.

The Queen of Hearts had talents and gifts she was apparently encouraged to polish and use to God's glory, and this she did with energy and proficiency that engendered praise from all who worked with her, or who benefited from her enterprises. She lost none of her femininity in the doing of it, balancing her ventures with womanly pursuits like the girdles she fashioned for the textile trade, and the clothes she sewed for her family. She mothered and wifed and loved her husband and kids as only a woman can, and excelled in all things. Now, I want to know how she did all of that, don't you?

Men of Quality Are Never Threatened by Women of Equality

It really is a male world, and I have often found myself struggling in this area. For example, being a woman in the pulpit has hardly been a feminine prerogative. How do you bring an authoritative word and retain your femininity? How do you say something you feel very strongly about—sweetly? As I began to find myself invited to take such opportunities of ministry, I began to pray God would help me never to be aggressive—or loud—or masculine. The Lord had painted me with the brush of femininity, and I asked Him to help me accomplish what He was leading me to do and not threaten the men as I did it. He

gave me the answer to my dilemma before I had hardly
begun to ask my questions. My very femininity gave me
the clue to the mystery. After all, only a woman knows
how to truly be a woman. God had made me a man-ess
quite different from a man and whatever I would do, that
difference would surely show. Women have an unbelievable sense of the feminine, because they have been
created that way. They really do know instinctively the
ways they can let men know they are glad that they are
women. They can also let it be known they are apprecia-
tive of the protection, caring, and respect of the male
species. God showed me ways of letting men know I was
not lording it over them, or usurping their authority, but
was in subjection to the headship of the particular fellowship of believers that had invited me to exercise my gifts,
to the edifying of the Church. It was largely a matter of
my attitude, not theirs!

Attitudes

If we are going to be working women in a man's world,
either from careful prayerful choice, or out of harsh necessity, we will need to work on our attitudes. What is our
attitude toward the men we work for because they are
men, for example? Perhaps we have had a bad experience
with a member of the opposite sex, and our bitterness
spills over to the men we meet in the workplace. Attitude
is everything—well, almost everything! Who wants to
work with anyone either in or outside of the home who
has a bad attitude? Our Queen of Hearts had a cheerful
attitude, working willingly with her hands. The Lord is
concerned with the attitudes we have. They are very important to Him. He asks us to serve Him with a willing
heart or not to bother serving Him at all. The Lord told
Moses to tell the Israelites that unless they brought a willing offering, they were not to bring one. "Speak unto the

children of Israel, that they bring me an offering: of every man that giveth it willingly with his heart ye shall take my offering" (Exodus 25:2). The Bible tells us that God loves a cheerful giver: "Every man according as he purposeth in his heart, so let him give; not grudgingly, or of necessity: for God loveth a cheerful giver" (2 Corinthians 9:7). If we give reluctantly or under compulsion, He is displeased with us. This principle, I may say, goes far beyond mere monetary offerings. "For if there be first a willing mind, it is accepted according to that a man hath, and not according to that he hath not" (2 Corinthians 8:12). So He tells us just in case we missed the point.

Attitudes! We need to ask ourselves, *Can I do this work with a cheerful and submissive attitude?* There are so many people in the workplace who give their time grudgingly, or of necessity, simply going through the motions of their jobs. What a difference when a Queen of Hearts arrives on the scene! What joy to be on the hospital ward or run a business with a workmate who has a cheerful attitude! That sort of spirit makes quite an impact on a society that is largely working for what it can get out of it, and not for what it can put into it. If we are out there doing our work "as unto the Lord and not unto men"— serving our employers—we are bound to be queens of our bosses' hearts!

> *Cheerful Givers—happy Givers,*
> *This the way my work shall be;*
> *Listening, learning, running, earning*
> *Serving only Thee!*

Motivation

Motivation has an awful lot to do with attitude. Paul, writing to the Ephesian Christians, said, "Let him that stole steal no more: but rather let him labour, working with his hands the thing which is good, that he may have to give to him that needeth" (Ephesians 4:28).

It does not say that he may "have to have," or that he may "have to have more," but that he may "have to give"! Since it is God who "giveth us power to get wealth" (*see* Deuteronomy 8:18), it follows that He holds us responsible as good stewards to give out of the fruits of our labors to those in need. *Those in need* may well be our own children, needing help to go to college, or a married son, requiring assistance in buying his own home; or it may be the refugees that have come to our city; or the retired people who have had their government grants cut—whatever—the Christian woman keeps all this in mind. With a cheerful, willing attitude she works hard that she may have—not to necessarily have more for herself but that she might "have to give."

I know a Christian girl who is married to an unbeliever. Her husband was understandably reluctant to spend any of their money on church-related causes. She asked him if he would mind her working every other week cleaning a woman's house for her, and if she could do what she liked with the money she earned. ("That she must have to give.") He had no objection, and so that is what she did —flying cheerfully around the home—a sheer ray of sunshine, doing hard housework "as unto the Lord." She also worked in a bank part-time—the rest of her days were given to the care of her husband and two small children. Another woman I know baby-sits by the same principle. Her earnings are given to Christian missions. Our attitude toward work should take into account our stewardship of time, talents, and earning power, and be related to God.

What we do with our extra earnings is very important. If our motivation to earn more money is that we might accumulate more things, we will not be very happy. After all ". . . a man's life consisteth not in the abundance of the things which he possesseth" (Luke 12:15). If we have a healthy theology concerning Christian stewardship, we will have little problem knowing how to use our earnings as He would have us use them.

But many of us are not going to have any extra money to use. Both of the partners' incomes will be necessary to survive, or perhaps one is a single parent. Yet I wonder about the level of that survival. Do we ever take time out to evaluate what our wants are and what are our needs? Don't you think we are in danger of getting them all mixed up? Perhaps we ought to ask ourselves just what is our motivation for working outside of the home in the first place?

Staying Power

If we do get back into the work force, motivation has a lot to do with our staying power, too. Many women have flocked back to work and are wishing that they hadn't. They are disappointed and disillusioned with the job opportunities they have found, or more correctly, *haven't* found out there. On the other hand, others are doing very well and, believe it or not, are wishing that they weren't! There is such a thing as job burnout, and it is a factor to be taken into consideration. My eye was caught by an article in a national newspaper entitled "Job Burnout Doesn't Always Wait for Middle Age." The article stated that burnout once associated with middle age is claiming a growing number of professionals in their twenties and thirties.

"We've been seeing more and more women who have had fast-track careers and who are often on the second marriage by the mid-thirties and up. Then they consider having a child. Given all the anxieties, the mistrust, the discrimination they face at work, many of these successful women are deciding to drop out and have babies." Not only that, "These women are working harder than many men around them, and they feel artificial limitations on how high they can go. It leads to a tremendous amount of frustration and burnout." (The *Sun,* San Bernardino, California, Wednesday, November 10, 1982, PAA-6.)

In one breath, the article says women *are* being successful, but in the next breath we are told there is a conflict and battle going on to achieve such success. All of us facing a decision to return to work need to think about "what price success?" If it means my marriage, my kids, my mental or physical health, it's not worth it. And if it means a dog-eat-dog climb to the top, taking on discriminatory attitudes and actions every rung of the ladder, that's not worth it to me. Can I stay the course? Can I retain my Christian testimony, my integrity, cling to a Christian work ethic, and all the time maintain a cheerful attitude? Can I, in other words, burn on instead of burning out?

I believe a Queen of Hearts who, after careful and prayerful consultation with the Lord, her family, and her friends, goes back to work with the right attitude and support, will, like the little burning bush in Moses' desert wilderness "be able to burn on and yet not be consumed" (*see* Exodus 3:2). When God's power fills us, we will be sustained, and I believe such a woman will know what it is to be a light in a dark place, where many need to be shown the way to Christ. But it has to be *worth* it! Once the novelty has worn off, it has to be worth all the blood, sweat, and tears, not to mention the wear and tear upon our families that it is going to take to stay the course.

Mount Up With Wings

"But where will we get all this inner strength, this staying power from?" you may ask. From the *Lord,* of course! Now you knew I would say that, didn't you? One of my favorite verses comes at the end of Isaiah, chapter 40: "But they that wait upon the Lord shall renew their strength; they shall mount up with wings as eagles; they shall run, and not be weary; and they shall walk, and not faint" (verse 31).

The secret is a waiting heart, an inner feasting that makes you strong inside—a place to run within that is private and precious because Jesus is there. You don't have to wait till you are going to bed at the end of the day to wait on the Lord. He is ready to meet you any moment you need renewing. He promises He will lift the weariness. He can do this because He is the unwearied God. He invigorates us because He is newness of life Himself. He is self-sustaining, vibrant power. As I learn to appropriate His unwearied liveliness, I will mount up with wings as the eagle, flying above my circumstances. I will run and not be weary—I will walk and not faint.

The Bible uses the picture of the eagle to illustrate renewal because it is one of the oldest living birds. Aristotle and Pliny believed it never died. Those that wait on the Lord will find their Spirit renewed like the eagles. We may die of all sorts of diseases, but God promises an inward resource that will lift our spirits above everything else, and even at the end of our days, our renewed soul will fly right into heaven. While we are still down here, however, we shall run—and get our second wind, we shall walk—and not faint.

The Christian working woman, pressured beyond measure, has to learn to wait on the Lord if she is to avoid burnout. Do we wait upon the fellowship of Christian books, the church, the wonderful friends we have, or do we wait first and foremost on the Lord? You never get weary with waiting but you surely do if you don't!

Profit or Loss

After all the wear and tear we will experience with having two jobs, we will want to come home at the end of the day with a profit in our pockets. That means we shall have to be good. The Queen of Hearts found "her industry was profitable!" (verse 18 MOFFATT). She excelled at what she did. No better girdles than hers on the market; no better wine from any other vineyard; no better deal on the land sales she negotiated. And there's nothing wrong with that. What is more, a good job deserves fair remuneration, and there's nothing wrong with that either.

When I said earlier that we should remember to "labor with our hands that we might 'have to give' and not necessarily to 'have to have,'" I didn't mean we should only earn money in order to give it all away. Our Queen of Hearts bought good clothes and provided wonderful material blessings for her family (verses 21, 22), but she held all that profit in trust. Whenever she saw a need outside her family circle, she responded by sharing out of her surplus—while at other times, no doubt she gave at cost to herself. There is absolutely nothing wrong with making a profit, as long as the love of money, which is the root of all evil (notice, please, it does not say "Money is the root of all evil" but the *"love* of it") (1 Timothy 6:10) does not corrupt us and steal our hearts away from the Lord.

Women are good. There is no question in my mind at all that women can do an equally good job as men, apart from tasks with severe physical limitations, such as laying concrete blocks! What is more, the statistics are beginning to agree. Women are emerging as heads of corporations; achieving prominence in otherwise previously male preserves; and being acknowledged as equal in job performance. But there's a problem I have already mentioned. Some men are frightened. They feel threatened by this invasion of their privacy, or maybe they are insecure themselves. Perhaps their cultural background screams out against the emerging woman in her new role. What is more, I have noticed that when a man is threatened, he tends to fight back with chauvinistic remarks.

"Because I'm a Woman!"

For example, let's take women in politics. Sixty-two years after winning the right to vote, more women than ever are running for office. Motivation to enter this field differs as widely as the women who enter it differ. Lynn Cutler, forty-four, admits she decided to take on Rep. Cooper Evans, *"because* I'm a woman. I want to see more women in office." But getting elected creates a whole new set of problems for women.

> In Chicago, Mayor Jane Byrne is notorious for her tart tongue which was often ascribed to her sex—not her personality. Some members of the male-dominated city council insist that Byrne is "menopausal," and . . . some aldermen suggest that Byrne is living proof of the fickleness of women.
> If [former Mayors] Dick Daley and Michael Bilandic changed their minds it was because they "reconsidered" and wisely changed direction, says Don Rose, a veteran political consultant who parted ways with Byrne after managing her campaign. "If Jane Byrne changes her mind, it's a sign she's unstable." *Newsweek,* November 1, 1982

A woman in the working world faces these sorts of things, and she has to be secure enough in herself and in her decision to be God's woman in God's world, doing God's work in God's way, to be able to laugh winsomely, and just get on with the job in hand—not as a competitor but as a collaborator. A Queen of Hearts knows how to do that. She knows how to work without losing her femininity, without competing, and without putting achievement above her relationships—either at home *or* at work. She knows how to do this because she is a Christian. She knows what it is to forgive. She knows if she becomes the butt of men's jokes because she is a woman, then that it is their problem, not hers. She knows she can get her affirmation from God. If it is not forthcoming from her boss, she can survive, knowing the Lord loves and appreciates her, because she is doing her work "as unto the Lord and not unto men." She believes her position at work depends upon the Lord and not upon the boss. Her job is to work hard at being faithful and loyal and do the very best that she can do. Then it is up to God to do what is best for her. She really trusts God to put her in the place *He* wants her to be. Then she can be as happy with promotion as without it.

Even a Queen of Hearts might well discover she is passed over because she is a woman, or because she is a Christian woman. She can possibly find herself with two strikes against her. If this is the case, she knows what to do because she's in the Word and has been memorizing 1 Peter 2:18–21 which says:

> Servants, be subject to your masters with all fear; not only to the good and gentle, but also to the froward. For this is thankworthy, if a man for conscience toward God endure grief, suffering wrongfully. For what glory is it, if, when ye be buffeted for your faults, ye shall take it patiently? but if, when ye do well, and suffer for it, ye take it patiently, this is acceptable with God. For even hereunto were ye called: because Christ also suffered

for us, leaving us an example, that ye should
follow his steps.

People Have to Matter More Than Promotion

But it isn't just the men who are frightened with the
wave of women threatening to engulf them—the women
who are already back at work are threatened too! "What
about the other women I have to work with out there?"
you may do well to ask. "What will I meet in the way of
'cat eat cat' competition if I start and do well with my
work?" That's a good question, and a very necessary one.
Being forewarned is forearmed.

Betty Friedan, quoting one of her co-workers said, "You
can't count on any woman not to sell other women out!
A woman will put achievement above relationships." Not
a Christian woman, Betty! Sometimes a personality conflict is unavoidable, but we cannot be responsible for
other people's actions—only our own. Ambition must be
tempered with the Spirit's grace, and attitude must be
governed by the Spirit's sweetness.

Real Men Don't Earn Less Than Their Wives—True or False?

A Queen of Hearts is watchful of her close relationships
in and out of the home. For instance, consider her husband—if she has one. What happens when a talented wife
works, does well, and begins to bring home a bigger pay-
check than her husband? This is happening with monoto-
nous regularity today and the repercussions can be
devastating to the marriage relationship. A number of
New York surveys commented on their findings this way,
"A man whose wife earns more than he does is a prime
candidate for a rotten love life, divorce, and early death!"
They found that with both partners working a marriage
was more likely to be a battlefield of psychological and

physical abuse than if the wife stayed home.

Another very interesting article from *Psychology Today* (November 1982), had a startling headline: REAL MEN DON'T EARN LESS THAN THEIR WIVES. In one out of ten American couples, the wife now earns more than the husband. "One-third of the husbands who earned less said that their love for their spouse outweighed her love for him or was unrequited . . . Those men said that their sex lives were in jeopardy."

So let's get down to business! Does a Queen of Hearts run the risk of alienating her husband and family, her friends and her workmates by going back to work? Yes, she does. Added to this, she also runs the risk of alienating her church. Many conservative congregations hold tenaciously to a "woman's place being in the home," as scriptural principle and philosophy, and can put pressure on the working wife and mother to reconsider her position. Part of their concern is very real and needs to be considered. Many people have severe misgivings about working mothers, while they have fewer reservations concerning women without families. The home is in danger of becoming just a house where strangers live together. There is no question about it—there is much to consider when small children are involved.

Awareness

If after considering all of these important things, you decide to go to work, you have to train yourself to be aware of the ongoing dangers—especially in your home. The Queen of Hearts "watches carefully all that goes on throughout her household . . ." (verse 27 TLB). RSV says, "She looks well to the ways of her household," while Moffatt renders the verse, "She keeps an eye upon her household . . ."! I like that. We must keep an eye on things. What things? Husbands for a start.

The Queen of Hearts watches everything and everybody in her household. She is well aware of the dangers of overload, and she keeps an eye open for signals of distress on the home front! *But what do you watch for,* you may wonder. Watch your husband's reaction when you start to do well. Is he pleased or is he threatened? It could be that he is insecure himself, and to see his wife do better than he, depresses him and creates a grudging, chronic resentment. He may try to hide it, but you can usually tell if anything is wrong. Listen to his statements. What does he really mean when he comes home at the end of a day, looks around a messy house and says, "What a mess. I'll help you tidy it up"? Is he saying, "Why don't you quit your job and stay home and sort it out"—or is he really wanting to help? The fact is, help will be needed in the house once a woman returns to work. The husband is going to have to lower his expectations of his wife as Supermom. She cannot be in two places at once, and yet many a man finds himself yearning for the good old days, when he didn't have to come home and help with the chores. He's tired, wants to put his feet up, and watch TV. He begins to wonder bitterly why it can't be the same as it used to be.

Communication

Good communication is therefore absolutely essential during the initial adjustment period and on an ongoing basis. In chapter 31 of Proverbs we hear the husband praising his Queen of Hearts for her excellent work. They (he and the children) are actually talking about it! Some men simply internalize their resentment and let it fester away, until it boils over in a flaming row. If there are real misgivings on one partner's part, maybe you could have a trial period. Perhaps after six months to a year, the husband could take the wife to a cozy restaurant and evaluate the experiment. If there is no option economically, and the wife has to work—the restaurant is still a very good idea! As you adjust to a whole new life-style together, you will be better able to adapt and share the new responsibilities if you can talk often and honestly together about your feelings. You'll also need to discuss the effect you both think your work schedule is having on the children.

Talk about your sex life, too. Does the wife flop into bed with nothing left to give? Does the husband pretend not to notice? Watch it carefully, and perhaps begin to build in an overnight in a hotel, or a romantic weekend without the kids once in a while. Remember the extra money you make can be used to enhance your own relationship which is perhaps under a new strain, as well as providing for the children's needs.

Listening

Listen to your children's conversation. Are you putting an unfair burden on them, now that you need them to do so much more housework, as well as all their homework? Before a friend of mine returned to work, the children (five teen-agers) were brought into the decision-making process, and a full and frank discussion ensued. Concerns were voiced around the kitchen table as to what was fair and what was unreasonable; what was wise and what was unwise; what was too much and what was too little. When Mom eventually did return to the work force, it was the whole family who decided it should be so, and they adjusted their individual expectations accordingly. Husbands shouldn't expect Mom to be a Supermom, and wives should not expect Dad to be a Superdad either. That's just not fair. Everybody will have to give a little. But a family that recognizes that Mom needs to return to the work force for the good of the whole family, senses a togetherness about the venture, and that excited support is essential for the working mother.

Watch younger children who cannot verbalize what they feel and if you see abnormal signs of behavior, adjust accordingly. When Stuart was traveling for long periods of time and I was working, our children were all under twelve years of age. Generally things went smoothly, but at one point Dave failed an important exam, and Judy began to sleepwalk the very night her daddy went away, sleeping naturally again as soon as he returned. The alert was sounded and Stuart and I regrouped. In fact, we moved three thousand miles, to a new country and a new job and a new chance to prioritize our family time. Sometimes it's Dad that has to adjust—as in this instance. Sometimes it's Mom that needs to stop working. On other occasions, it's the growing children who have to stretch and reach and grow up to new responsibilities, as they do their part.

I am convinced children must be part of it though. I have seen far too many mothers baby their kids, and not ask for any involvement from them at all. It's as if they dare not ask them to take responsibility at home, in case they resent her going back to work, and she has to stop! The balance of fair and reasonable jobs and overload for the children of working mothers forever remains a touchy subject. Each family has to mount guard as the Queen of Hearts did, keeping an eye on *everything*. As the pivot of her family circle, I think a woman is in a marvelous position to see the danger signals clearly, and I believe it is up to her to sound the warning bell when it is is needed.

Limp Loins

Not only does a Queen of Hearts have to keep an eye on her husband and on her children, she has to keep an eye on herself! Do you know your own capabilities physically, psychologically, and emotionally? The Queen of

Hearts "girdeth her loins with strength, and strength-eneth her arms" (verse 17). She knew she had to be physically fit to keep such a demanding schedule. This subject of physical exercise is a matter of knowing yourself. Some can play racquetball, others swim, some do aerobics, others golf, and a few can only manage a slow shuffle around the block with the dog! Know yourself and don't overdo, but do do *something!* And try to do it every day. Gird your loins with strength.

Too many women have limp loins, if you'll excuse the expression! How out of shape we are. We will never be queen of the working world if we don't shape up. The Queen of Hearts was energetic and a hard worker, "rising up while it was yet night" (*see* verse 15).

Delegation

The Queen of Hearts did not rise up while it was yet night because her conscience wouldn't let her sleep either. She rose up early in the morning to prepare her food for her household and to delegate the day's duties to her maidens. Preparation and delegation are vital if you are to be queen of everybody's hearts. And the key to preparation and delegation is *information.* People need their job description spelled out for them. When we tell our children (our maidens) to "Set the table when you come home from school, please," that is not enough by itself. We should tell them what china to use, whether to put ice in the glasses, if small or large forks are needed—in other words, we should spell out the details. Information is important where tasks are concerned. This way we avoid heated recriminations when we come home tired and weary and find the job half-done! Leave notes, make lists, put up posters, have family powwows, but make sure the information you want communicated to your family members is clearly understood. And don't be afraid to delegate. Obviously, the job would be better done if you could do it, but if you will not be around when it needs doing, you have no alternative but to delegate it. This way children learn responsibility and skills they will use in years to come in their own homes, and our menfolk learn to care for themselves if the need should ever arise.

Mechanical Maidens

Put your maidens to work! "But I'm not wealthy—I don't have maidens," you wail! We *all* have maidens. Silent maidens they may be—but here in the USA what home is without a mechanical maiden? A washer or dryer, a toaster or electric can opener, a garbage disposal, or a vacuum cleaner. All stand obediently around our homes, waiting patiently for us to put them to work. None of that sort of help was available to our Queen of Hearts, so she used human help. But we have marvelous aids around us in our twentieth-century homes. Make sure you put them to use! Delegate. Make them serve you and save your precious time. Learn to use and properly care for them. One-half of the problem is we don't know how to organize our help. Don't be too proud to look around and find a friend whose house is immaculate and ask her to tell you how it is done. How does she use her mechanical maidens? I'm sure you will find out your friend is good at preparation, delegation, and information. Keep a schedule. Buy a diary you can carry with you. List things you need to do. Check them off when they are done. Manage your time, and don't let your time manage you! You'll need to delegate to somebody if you work outside the home. The Queen of Hearts provided food for her household and tasks for her maidens.

Management doesn't mean you do nothing, you know. It means it frees you up to do something else.

Pray About It

Let me finish with a word of guidance to those of you contemplating going back to work.

Take time out to pray about it. Ask the Lord to show you what to do. If He is Lord of your life, He will have an opinion about the matter and you will need to find out what it is. "How do I do that?" you ask. By reading the Bible. Read a portion every day. Look for principles to guide you. A friend of mine was left by her husband, who disappeared without a trace. With no child support coming in, it was obvious she needed to work. She came from a sincere but I believe misguided family who exhorted her to "trust the Lord" for daily bread, stay home with her children, and see how God would look after her. Searching the Scriptures, torn between her basic, cultural, Christian heritage and common sense, she came across the verse, "But if any provide not for his own, and specially for those of his own house, he hath denied the faith, and is worse than an infidel" (1 Timothy 5:8).

Realizing she was the provider through no choice of her own, she received a clear imperative to return to the world and work. From now on she would need to be buying the "daily bread." Ask your friends' advice. Invite their Christian counsel, but make sure you ask people who know you and your children well, and who understand your situation. Listen carefully to what they have to say. Also you can make a list of the pros and cons of all of the alternatives and advice offered to you, and see which is the longest. It's a good idea to ask the elders of your church to guide you, too.

If you have a husband, make sure that this is a *joint* decision. His job is to "nourish and cherish you" as Christ does the church (*see* Ephesians 5:29). The word *nourish* used here means to help you discover your God-given talents and abilities and make sure you use them. The word *cherish* means to protect you while you do so. The husband is told to dwell with his wife according to knowledge. And so he needs to know you so thoroughly, he can take the pressure off when you need him to; lower his expectations at other times; and trust you to "have a go," spread your wings and fly at the right moment. Do ask your husband. Make sure you do this together, and evaluate the situation often to see what it is doing to your relationship.

If your children are old enough to have any input, ask them for it. Listen carefully to what they say. Ask them to pray about it. Take them into your confidence, and explain why you are thinking of such a change. After all, their little lives are to be drastically affected by your decision.

"Don't Baby-sit Us!"

When I began to accept invitations to speak, which necessitated my traveling, I turned to the women in our church fellowship to help me with baby-sitting. Not that our children were babies anymore. Dave was fourteen, and Judy twelve, and Pete ten. After one memorable weekend, when the children gave the young couple we had invited to care for them a real runaround, we had it out in a family powwow. "Why can't we stay by ourselves?" Dave asked me. "How can you ask such a thing?" I replied. "If you had shown yourselves responsible, maybe we would have given you some responsibility!" Stuart, however, suggested we try it—just once. "Remember the street work we used to do with the mission," he reminded me. "We gave the young rascals responsibility before they showed us they deserved it, and it made many of them shape up and be responsible. Let's take the risk." So we did, and it really worked out well.

The children rose to the occasion and responded well to the chance we gave them. They felt "adult" and "trusted" and that sat well with their egos.

Then you need to know if you can *really* be honest with yourself. What is your reason for going back to work? Is it clean and right and good? Is it a holy and high motivation? Can you pray to the Lord,

> *Throw light into the darkened cells*
> *Where passion reigns within,*
> *Quicken my conscience till it feels*
> *The loathesomeness of sin*

and mean it?

If you can and if you do, and if you seek light upon the question with a clear conscience and a pure heart, God will delight to tell you the answer. Then once the answer is given—obey it! Whether it be to stay home or return to work, go for it with all your might. If it be to return to the working world when all else is in place, you will find God will help you to be queen of the traders' hearts, and that will bring glory to His Name.

If it be to stay home at this time and minister there, do it and find that "in acceptance lieth peace." Each family relationship is unique, and each has its own dynamic. The blending of differing personalities into a corporate whole is what family is all about. The family, after all, is a vital building block of society, and I believe that society is only strong when the marriage bond is held in honor, and the children are raised with love and in the nurture and admonition of the Lord.

The Empty Nest

A last word to those who have the option to stop working, or to those whose children have left home. You may find yourselves strangely at a loss to know what to do! Getting a job is not the only alternative. Voluntary Christian service is a marvelous option. For those of us who choose to do with less material things and use our full-time energies for His Kingdom's sake, the opportunities are legion. I thank God for such an option offered to me. I have worked ever since we got married. Stuart and I decided we would manage with one income—his, and this has given me freedom to develop a Christian ministry. There has been some unexpected remuneration here and there, but it has never been asked for. I have sought to make no charge for the Gospel, and have used Stuart's salary and my book money to pay my own way to minister around the world. There are many people who cannot afford to pay my way, and I thank God for the chance I have to go to them anyway and encourage them in the Lord. This was a deliberate and joint decision before God that Stuart and I made over twenty-five years ago, and I would like to go on record that I would not have had it any other way. It has meant I have learned what the working woman is up against (as I have been out and about in a man's world), and yet I have lived my life in voluntary Christian service—a fantastic experience. May I suggest that that is a royal and rare privilege—a huge joy. Try it —you'll like it!

This may be a very viable alternative for some of you reading these pages. Are you a teacher? Teach for Him. A secretary? You are needed on the mission field or in the home office. Do you have administrative skills? God's Kingdom needs such to serve it. Working for heavenly wages beats anything else I know, and if God should so call you—happy will you be. A few of us should heed our Lord's words, "Lift up your eyes [from material considerations], and look on the fields; they are white already to harvest" (John 4:35).

Being available full time for God's service, when we have attained a little wisdom concerning life and hopefully a measure of Christian maturity, means we have a chance to bring some eternal blessings into people's lives. There is no satisfaction on earth that can match that experience. Once the children leave the nest, they make room for a whole lot of productive ideas we can hatch and nurture for Christ and His Kingdom, and for those of us that face those possibilities, we should at the very least pray about them.

For those of us who feel strongly that God has surely led us into the marketplace, let me exhort you to be *salt*, arresting corruption and light in a dark place. To be queen of the merchants' hearts will undoubtedly bring glory to His Name!

WORKSHEET

Read these points to ponder from chapter 6 and spend five minutes doing so.

- If you don't know how to help the house help, that's not going to help the house.

- Ambition must be tempered by the Spirit's grace, and attitude must be governed by the Spirit's sweetness.

- Men of quality are not threatened by women of equality.

- Real men don't earn less than their wives—true or false?

- Too many people have limp loins, if you'll excuse the expression! How out of shape we are. We will never be queen of the working world if we don't shape up.

- Watch younger children who cannot verbalize what they feel, and if you see abnormal signs of behavior, adjust accordingly.

- Once the children leave the nest, they make room for a whole lot of productive ideas we can hatch and nurture for Christ and His Kingdom.

• I have lived my life in voluntary Christian service—a fantastic experience. May I suggest that that is a royal and rare privilege—a huge joy.

• Take time out to pray about returning to work. Ask the Lord what His opinion is.

1. **Write a Sentence Answering Each Question.**
   a) What did she do?
   b) How did she do it?
   c) Why did she do it?
   d) Should I do it?

2. **Do YOU Think Women Should Work Outside the Home?** Give *your* reasons.

3. **For the Christian Woman**
   Make a list of ten guidelines for the Christian woman from this chapter.
   1.
   2.
   3.
   4.
   5.
   6.
   7.
   8.
   9.
   10.

4. **Especially for You**
   Which part of the lesson or verse of Scripture spoke to you and why?

5. **Pray About It.**

QUEEN OF THE LORD'S HEART

*. . . a woman that feareth the
Lord, she shall be praised.*

Verse 30

Acceptance

WHAT WOMAN DOES NOT SEEK ACCEPTANCE,
appreciation and affirmation? "What must I do to be
praised?" cries today's woman. Even the woman who
prides herself on being self-sufficient, looks for these very
things. She accepts, appreciates, and affirms herself continually. To her, liberty means looking out for Number
One. She is the Alpha and Omega, the beginning and the
end of her existence. She is also the author and finisher of
her faith. She writes her own so-called bible and makes
her own rules and is careful to say, "Well done, thou good
and faithful servant" at the end of the day. She has made
herself her own god, and therefore freely forgives herself
anything and everything she does. She delights to pray, "I
forgive me" and basks in the pseudopeace that ensues
when one chloroforms one's conscience and settles for less
than God's best. She seeks to answer her own prayers, and
when unsuccessful, blames other people. She is never
wrong. She is proud, though she never would admit to it,
as pride never admits to anything that puts him or her in
the wrong light.

Pride

Pride doesn't fear the Lord because he doesn't fear anyone. Or, so he says. He certainly acts as if he fears neither man nor beast. But then pride wins the devil's Academy Award for Best Actor, because the devil is the source of pride, and he rewards his own. Pride lies through his teeth, is a hypocrite who is proud to be seen in the right places (like church) and is desperately lonely. He sings solo whenever he gets the chance, because he can't stand the competition of duet or trio. He never joins the choir, since there are far too many people to share the applause. He preens—is prickly, peevish, and oh, so poor, having robbed himself of the true nobility of humility that is wealth indeed. Millions of light-years ago, when the devil left heaven in a hurry (pride always comes before a fall, you know), he determined to worship only himself and to crusade for converts. He's been busy ever since, and highly successful, convincing thousands of people that if they don't enjoy the worship of God down here, they will never be happy in heaven.

Heaven's Just Like Church

"Why," he whispers in their ears, "heaven is just like that boring church you go to. It's the sort of place you'll find yourself sitting on a cushionlike pink, damp cloud in a heavenly pew, playing a harp for all eternity. You will have to listen to everlasting sermons on how wicked you are, too. You don't need *that* now, do you?" he'll ask. "You're all right, you know," he'll say. "I think you're really quite a good person inside. You don't need God's help or anyone else's assistance in the whole wide world—you don't even need *my* help to be totally self-sufficient!"

In the end, the old serpent has people believing that fearing God means all of the above negatives, plus being eternally terrified. After Satan succeeds in making people do what he did—become independent of God—he goes on his diabolical way, viciously confident that he has everlasting company.

The devil tries to make you fear that God will take your independence away and ruin your life, because he wants you to believe dependence on God is a minus and not a plus.

"Fear God, by all means," he says, sagely. "You rightly fear that old spoilsport!"

But this is not what fearing God is all about.

Contrition Is a Place You Go

You see, fearing God means we rightly fear His holiness, as we see we have come far short of the high standard He has set for us. That standard is absolute rightness. Knowing we have fallen far short of His requirements should make us fear His judgment.

Fearing God doesn't stop there. It drives us to our knees in true contrition. Contrition is the place you go when you are really, really sorry about your sins and shortcomings (or coming shorts), and where you will find a nail-pierced hand, resting on your head, telling you it's going to be all right.

Somewhere in the shadows outside the safe circle of His love you'll hear the old devil gnashing his teeth because he's lost you—but that's a lot better than you gnashing *yours* because he's found you, don't you think?

Your Choice

You see, you can choose whether you want to go to heaven while you're still here on earth. In fact, the choice *has* to be made this side of the grave; you can't make it later. The Bible says, "It is appointed unto men once to die, but after that the judgment" (Hebrews

9:27). You can choose to belong to your father, the devil, or choose to belong to your Father, the Lord! It's quite simple and straightforward, really. Actually, the Bible says we are all of our father, the devil (John 8:44; 1 John 3:10) until we cry to God to rescue us and adopt us into His family as His sons (Galatians 4:5). We all have the devil's likeness written all over our characters since the day we were born.

Self-righteousness

We can even be religious and be of our father, the devil! Jesus Christ faced some very religious people one day and told them that very thing. Because Christ was God, He knew what was in man. He discerned the devices and desires of the hearts. That's how He knew the Pharisees were going about to kill Him. "Ye are of your father the devil," He said to them, and, ". . . He was a murderer from the beginning . . . " (John 8:44).

Jesus told a story in Luke 18:10–14 about a man who sounds just like that. He went to church to pray, and thank God that he was not like other men. He was pleased with himself for helping the poor and felt he was a good Pharisee, doing all the acceptable things acceptable Pharisees do. He was, in fact, proud he wasn't a sinner like "this other man," who was also at prayer in the temple. "This other man" he was referring to happened to be a publican; a despised Jew who had sold his soul to Rome and collected taxes for the government, fleecing the rich, oppressing the poor, and feathering his own nest along the way. But the publican knew well what he was. He was a sinner! He was of his father, the devil. What's more, he rightly feared God. "Father, forgive me," he prayed brokenly. Shattered by what he was doing, convicted about the sort of person he had become, he sought God's forgiveness and the power to be different.

Jesus explained that both of these men were sinners. One had a religious life-style, the other an irreligious life-style. Both were of their father, the devil, for both were thieves at heart. Did not the Pharisee steal the glory due to God and apply it to himself? "I thank thee, God," he said. But Jesus reminded His hearers that the man stood and prayed thus "with himself" (verse 11). He was his own god. He freely forgave himself anything that was necessary and thanked himself that he was better than others; certainly better than this despised publican. The publican was a sinner, too. He had oppressed the poor, but he was wise. Wiser than the clever Pharisee who had had the opportunity of book learning. He had the wisdom to know that the "fear of the Lord is the beginning of wisdom . . ." (Psalms 111:10). He rightly acknowledged he needed to have a healthy attitude toward the holiness of God. He must cast himself on God's mercy and plead for His forgiveness if he was to be saved from the just deserts of his deeds. "I tell you," said Jesus, "this man went down to his house justified rather than the other: for every one that exalteth himself shall be abased; and he that humbleth himself shall be exalted" (verse 14).

The God of This World

A man or a woman who fears the Lord knows he or she is accountable to the Creator God. Satan, the father of pride and lies and murder, and all that is evil, is the god of *this* world. He is the lesser god. His avowed intent is to get God's creatures who live in God's rebellious world to live without God and worship him, instead. He wants us to live in constant fear of him. He wants to do to us what he did to our forefathers in Eden, present an alternative to the obedience and worship of God. But he's not stupid. He knows we know better than that, so he suggests we worship ourselves. If that approach is still too obvious, he will try anything and everything he can think up in his twisted, yet brilliant mind, to make us fear or worship other things. As long as we do not fall at the feet of Jesus Christ, as Thomas did, crying, "My Lord and my God," he is content.

The Praise of Men

Knowing the need of the human heart for the praise and affirmation that satisfies, Satan tries to stop us from seeking God's praise and offers a substitute—the praise of men. This is another twist to the problem. Our Queen of Hearts was praised by men. Her husband praised her, her children called her blessed. The merchants perceived her merchandise was good, and they bought it from her. Her good works praised her in the gates. The most subtle temptation of all is to allow the praise of men to become more important to us than the praise of God. We have no indication our proverbial lady ever allowed that to happen, but the temptation must have been there. Human beings must come to God through Christ and be accepted of Him. God will then affirm and appreciate them. His acceptance will set them free to accept other people's praise and keep it in the right perspective.

The church suffers from this seeking of earthly praise. People will withhold their service if they cannot have the visible place. If no one notices their hard work, their hard work will stop. We humans find it most difficult to render an act of service without being center stage to make it worth our while.

The Praise of Peers

"Isn't it more important what your loved ones think of you than what God thinks of you?" Satan whispers in our ear. Peer pressure is not only the teen-ager's problem! If Satan can get an unbelieving husband to praise his wife for drinking, smoking dope, or wearing seductive clothes, so he can show her off to his friends, he stands a good chance of getting a believing wife to succumb to the praise of man, rather than pursue the praise of God. After all, there's power in praise!

No Praise

Then, if Satan fails in using the praise of men to get us to do the wrong thing, he tries a famine of praise. "Try doing without it, then," he snarls! A woman who fears the Lord does not always engender everybody's praise. Unfortunately, doing what is good and what is right is not always doing the thing that is acceptable in men's eyes. If people are marching to a different drummer, there's bound to be a clash. And yet a grudging respect is often afforded the woman who fears the Lord. Who she is and what she does has to bring a reluctant acknowledgement from even the most hardened of hearts, although they will seldom let her hear it.

Consider Jesus Christ, for instance. Even His enemies said nice things about Him—doubtless behind His back! They praised His works. (They could not get by them.) His works praised Him in the gates. It was an indisputable fact that "He went around doing good." His good deeds spoke for Him, when men would not allow Him to speak for Himself. His acts of mercy and His clever teachings were well documented. "Never man spoke like this man," said the soldiers who had been sent to arrest Him and returned empty-handed. Some said things with chagrin; others with surprised joy; but say them, they did! What you do, because you love and fear the Lord, will bring respect if not praise. You may even get killed for your testimony to Christ just as they killed the Lord Jesus, but it will get to them because they well know that you are right. When someone truly fears the Lord and shows it by living a godly life, the very works this Christian will go about doing will bring praise at the gates!

Maybe that doesn't help *you* when you are the one who is the recipient of such poor respect. Let's face it, we had better learn how to get our praise and affirmation from God if we are to live like a Queen of Hearts before men, because the praise of men will unhappily not always be forthcoming.

The Praise of God

Consider Mary, the Mother of our Lord, for instance. She certainly was God's Queen of Hearts because she loved, reverenced, and served Him with all her soul! She feared God more than she feared anyone else in the world. She had lots of reasons to think twice when the angel came to greet her with the news that she was to bear God's Son! She knew fear, all right, and the devil attacked her for all he was worth, you may be sure. She must have feared the men of her village, who could have stoned her for adultery. According to their law and custom, they considered her married to Joseph. She must have feared what Joseph would do, knowing he would be the last to praise her for having someone else's baby. She certainly must have feared the priests at the temple and the local dignitaries at the synagogue who could well deal harshly with her. She must have feared the disgrace she would bring on her family. Mary must have known what it was to fear men. I'm sure she was smart enough to know that not one person would believe her wild story of angels and God-given babies, and therefore, none would praise her for fearing God and doing His will! But she feared God first, anyway, saying, "Behold the handmaiden of the Lord; be it unto me according to thy word" (Luke 1:38). She praised and worshiped God, and He praised her for praising Him! ". . . thou that art highly favoured . . ." the angel told her, "the Lord is with thee [even if no one else is!]: blessed are thou among women" (verse 28).

Encouragement

And then God in His grace sent Mary one little piece of encouragement along the way. Dear Elizabeth greeted her with praise. Mary's cousin, Elizabeth, was having a baby the "right" way, but God had apparently whispered in her ear that Mary was, too. When the ostracized, teenage girl knocked on the door of her much older cousin's house, she was greeted as a true Queen of Hearts would greet another Queen of Hearts. "Blessed is she that believed: for there shall be a performance of those things which were told her from the Lord" (verse 45). (It takes one to know one, you know.)

Mary was accepted and affirmed and appreciated by Elizabeth and that must have helped a great deal; but in the end, it had to be enough for Mary that she had pleased and honored God.

A woman who fears the Lord fears Him more than she fears anyone else on earth—not in the sense of being terror-stricken, but in the sense of having such a healthy reverence and respect for Him, and such a hatred of evil or anything that would displease Him—that this motivates all of her actions.

Sometimes, as in Proverbs 31, the woman ended up being everyone's Queen of Hearts. The praise of men flowed freely. But remember again, we are reading about the *ideal* woman stimulating the so-called ideal response. In the case of Mary, the praise of men was not the result of virtue, and yet the Lord leaned out of heaven and said, "You are *My* Queen of Hearts, Mary," and that was enough.

When the King of Hearts of the Proverbs 31 lady said, ". . . a woman that feareth the Lord, she shall be praised" (verse 30), he made a true statement. God will praise such a woman, whether anyone else ever gets around to it or not! Strangely enough, those of us who have been there know that that heavenly encouragement is worth all the discouragements put together.

When God Says "Thank You"

Most of our lives we concentrate on the fact that we must affirm our faith in God and appreciate Him. It's quite different to think of God affirming His faith in us, and appreciating us. It's a new concept for many of us that He can be pleased with us at all! But it's a good concept! Once a human being has been on his knees and felt the hand of God upon his head in praise, he will never be the same again. There is nothing that makes you feel quite so loved, warm, and complete as when God says, "Thank you." No matter if all the world rejects you—His word of affirmation is enough. We must learn to live our lives looking for that word.

When I was a young girl and at college in England, Billy Graham came to hold a crusade in London. A way was devised whereby "relay" services could be transmitted to churches all over the country. Those of us who lived in the midlands and up north could all be part of the excitement, even though we lived hundreds of miles away. I had only been a Christian for a very short time, but I took the training that was offered in order to counsel people. I worried that I didn't know enough. Why, it was only a short time ago that I had wondered if an apostle was the wife of an epistle! Would I be able to do the important and delicate work I was expected to do?

The British Way of Doing Things

The pastor of the church where we were having the meetings was very nice, but he made it clear he wasn't sure if he approved of the whole venture. "This Billy Graham is too American for my liking," he said. "It's not the British way of doing things. For example, the crusade team has asked that we invite people in the church to come forward at the end of Dr. Graham's message."

"What for?" I asked in amazement.

"To accept Jesus Christ as their Saviour," he replied. "And that's where you come in," he continued, looking at me very solemnly! "You, and all the other counselors we are training. You will get up and follow someone your own age and sex down the aisle and assist them with their questions." Then he added dubiously, "I have a certain distaste for the showiness of it all."

Fighting City Hall

That the man had a distaste for the whole concept of evangelism became very obvious to me as the classes progressed. My fellow counselors all seemed very mature and wise but began to reflect his skepticism, having severe doubts as to whether or not this was the way to do things. One of the men muttered, "Well, I think we ought to make it as hard as we possibly can so that only the 'real' ones show up at the front." I was appalled. Shouldn't we make it as easy as possible? After all, it was going to be as hard as it could be to leave a husband or a wife or a teen-age son sitting in the pew, and walk all alone to the front of the church, saying, "Here I am and here I stand, for I can do no other," without fighting city hall every step of the way! However, being by far the youngest Christian in that august group, I decided to keep quiet and wait and see what happened.

The first day of the crusade the great choir sang, a testimony was given, and then Dr. Graham spoke. I was riveted to my seat. The Holy Spirit was at work. I could hardly stand it! I looked furtively around me, superconscious of the big counselor's badge that seemed to fill my chest! The committee, true to their word, had made it as hard as they possibly could! The church they had chosen for the meetings was very long and narrow and had at least five steps up to a large platform that led to another smaller platform that led to yet another. They had carefully filled the choir stalls with teen-agers who were giggling and gawking at the congregation that faced them. The leaders of the meeting sat on eight chairs—like the elders in heaven, except they all had the most solemn, embarrassed, and disapproving faces (hardly like the elders in heaven, I am sure!). *No one will ever walk down that aisle,* I decided! But then Dr. Graham was preaching such a powerful sermon! *If only he could ask them to come forward, it would be all right,* I thought.

Here Am I—Send Me

Just as the message ended and before Dr. Graham gave the appeal, the leader of the local crusade committee leaped to his feet and, to my horror, switched off the sound. *Oh, no,* I thought, *he's going to do it himself!* I was right. Mumbling into his ecclesiastical collar, he suggested everyone was free to come to the front onto the platform if they wanted to accept Christ. The beautiful music was gone and an ominous silence filled the air. No one moved. No one breathed. But oh, I knew there had to be some there—some like me, who needed Jesus so badly that they must want to respond. There had to be some who didn't know where to find the courage to get up out of their seats and ask for help! I remembered Janet, the girl who had led me to Christ, asking me three questions: "Do you need Him, do you want Him, will you receive Him?" I had said yes to all of these queries but had blurted out, "But Janet —just how does He get inside me?" It was then she had prayed with me, suggesting I make that prayer my own

—"Jesus, I need You, Jesus, I want You—come into my heart!" I had said it fervently and sincerely after her and He had answered! If only I could help others to pray that prayer. Looking at the faces around me—I saw a mother ragged with worry, a businessman with his stiff British upper lip trembling, a teen-ager with the giggles wiped off her face, as a new hope dawned—but I knew there was no way they were going to make it down that aisle, and who could blame them—not I! With my heart pounding, I heard the voice of the Lord, "Whom shall I send and who will go for us?" I knew it was God's voice—why, had I not just read those very words that very morning from Isaiah's beautiful book? "Here am I, send me," I gulped into my program. "Go on, then," He said cheerfully, "down the aisle you go! If you make a move, they will; they just need someone to show them the way!"

The Longest Walk of My Life

The enormity of what I knew I must do overwhelmed me. There I was, with my counselor's badge stuck on my chest, proclaiming to all I was already converted. The pastor had made it abundantly clear he was not expecting anybody to respond, anyhow, and would be highly relieved if they didn't! What was more, our instructions had been explicit. I had been told in no uncertain terms to "follow" someone. "Wait till they go!" I had been told. The pounding of my heart sounded like a war drum in the jungle. At last, I gathered up my good intentions, stepped out into the aisle, and began the longest walk of my life. Eventually I stood—all alone right in the middle of the highest platform in floods of tears! But oh, the relief! I cannot describe the peace I found as I took my place. There was nothing to be relieved about in the faces around me, however! The teen-agers collapsed in hysterics, the elders on their thrones were suitably horrified, and the ominous silence grew more ominous still! No other feet had followed me down that aisle, and still I stood there. I don't think anyone knew what on earth to do! I didn't know what to do, either, but I didn't care. God was busy saying things like "I love you for this, Jill—thank you."

Joy Over Sinners Repenting

Facing the audience, gloriously free within, and perfectly composed—wetly but perfectly—I saw to my utter joy, people beginning to move forward, and was just in time to greet the thirty or forty folks who joined me on my "high hill." Among them were the businessman whose stiff upper lip was now in serious trouble, the teen-ager whose pluck in leaving friends in the chair stalls was incredible to me, and the ragged, worried mother. They didn't notice me, of course—they were coming to meet with God! They didn't thank me, either—why should they? They must have thought I was an unconverted counselor or something, and the committee certainly didn't appreciate my action. They let me know in a few cryptic comments exactly what they thought—in fact, I was expelled from the inquiry room in disgrace! But, oh, joy, what matter? The job was done, the help had been offered, the awkwardness broken, the sinners saved, and oh, joy, God was saying, "Thank you!" Walking home under the stars that night, singing at the top of my voice, I remember feeling more accepted, affirmed, and appreciated than I had ever been before! At last, after consistently doing the wrong thing all of my life, I had actually done the right thing, and I knew it!

You know something? There's a *difference* between *feeling good* about yourself and *worshiping* yourself. I've tried to explain that in the first chapter of this book. You feel good about yourself when you fear and reverence the

Lord and do what He wants you to do. You can accept yourself then, even when no one else accepts you, because the affirmation to your spirit is going on internally. "His Spirit bears witness with our Spirit that we are the children of God." "You belong to your Father, the Lord, not your father, the devil," the Spirit whispers to us. "You have showed Me you love the King by your actions. See, you are a true child of God."

The King of Hearts

This book has been mainly about the Queen of Hearts. Nothing has been said except in passing, concerning her King. In reality, he does not come into the picture much in the text. We can see the kind man in the shadows appreciating and affirming his wife, but in these last pages, I would like to look beyond the perfect man described for Lemuel by the queen mother, and use him as a picture of the King of Hearts in heaven. If I am to be queen of the Lord's heart, then I need to know just what that means. What is my heavenly husband like, and what will it take to please Him?

The King Is Excellent

First, the King of Hearts we have been thinking about in the Book of Proverbs not only commended his wife for excellence, but he excelled himself. He was "known in the gates, when he sitteth among the elders of the land" (verse 23). He was a leader of the people, a prominent person. And so is our King of Hearts in heaven. He is afforded the prominent place there because He is worthy! He sitteth among the elders of the land and "The four and twenty elders fall down before him that sat on the throne, and worship him that liveth for ever and ever, and cast their crowns before the throne, saying, Thou art worthy, O Lord, to receive glory and honor and power: for thou hast created all things, and for thy pleasure they are and were created" (Revelation 4:10,11).

Because He is excellent, He appreciates excellence in the creatures He created. Excellence gives Him pleasure. Just as the Proverbs 31 wife brought joy to her husband's heart because she excelled, so we can know we please our heavenly Husband's heart, when we reach beyond ourselves to do our very best for Him. Have you ever been given an *A* in school? Our daughter has grown up in the shape of the letter! "Judy doesn't know what it is to get a *B*," grumbled her brothers, as the semester ended and the report cards arrived. "Nor do you," replied Stuart with a grin. That wasn't altogether true, but Judy had certainly excelled. She has never known what it is not to be at the top. Sometimes she has had to crawl there on her hands and knees, but she has put up the flag on the summit of the Everest of her accomplishments over and over again, and we have sought to praise her for that.

If we would hear our Lord's praise, we must strive for the *A* as well. We must seek to excel as He excelled. We must do our best. Whatever has happened to the desire for excellence? We don't reach for a star anymore. Whether it be in sloppy workmanship or jobs half-done, or tasks abandoned when the going gets tough, or courses dropped when the demands get great, we don't bother to try very hard. A *C* will do when we are perfectly capable of getting an *A*. Now I know all of us cannot get an *A* in math, or literature, or football or art—but there is one subject we can all get an *A* in, if we choose to, and that is an *A* for effort. We can decide to go for the *A* when it comes to being queen of our heavenly King's heart. We can all do that. Intelligence, education, background, or privilege have nothing to do with this. Everyone of us has a chance to be or not to be like Him. Jesus speaking of His heavenly Father said, . . . "I do *always* those things that please him" (John 8:29, *italics added*), and we can strive to say the same.

A Crisis and a Process

But what does it take to excel? To excel in spiritual things may necessitate a crisis, which will institute a process that will go on for the rest of our lives.

The crisis comes when we realize that we have a choice to treat the King as King. If He is King, then He should be *my* King. Now that faces us with a crisis of conscience. To acknowledge Him as King of my life will mean He gives the orders, signs the decrees, makes the decisions, rules—and reigns supreme. "As in heaven—so on earth! In all things," as Paul says, "He must have the preeminence" (*see* Colossians 1:16,18). Paul did not say, "In some things, or in nearly everything," but, "in *all* things." Now that little word *all* can face us with a spiritual crisis. If the Lord be King and I His queen, then that heavenly relationship has to supersede all others. Whether it be my relationship with my husband, my children, my church, or my friends, He will come first. Once I have decided that, the process begins—the process that goes on for the rest of our days. Moment by moment and day by day, we will have to choose to please God, rather than men. We will have to choose to do what is good and right, rather than what is convenient and acceptable. That means we shall have to know what the good and the right act is that we must do, and that will lead us to a process of learning His Word. It will mean taking time out to spend time in the Bible. It will mean excelling at knowing the Scriptures.

I don't mean we will compete with others ("I know more than you" type of expression) but it means we will hand our tests back to Him and pray the prayer at the end of Psalm 139 that says, "Search me, O God, and know my heart: try me, and know my thoughts: And see if there be any wicked way in me, and lead me in the way everlasting" (verses 23, 24). He's the One that will correct our mistakes, enlighten our minds, and instruct our wills. It means being determined to excel in virtuous character. Submitting to my heavenly King will result in fruit on the trees of our actions, displayed in the orchards of our world. The union of His life with my life will produce patience, love, joy, self-control, and meekness this year, next year, and all the years, until we see Him face-to-face. If God is King of our hearts, mediocre Christian living will not be acceptable to Him or to us. It will be all or nothing. In the words of one of my favorite pioneer missionaries, who set off on an extremely dangerous assignment with a spring in his step and a smile on his face, "I'm going to do this for Him because years ago I said 'It is for Jesus—and it's for keeps.' " It means laying down my life, my loves, my everything, and that's all right. If it means going anywhere, anytime, anyplace, is that all right with you? Making sure the King of your heart is King means spiritual excellence, not lukewarm love. It means, in the famous words of C. T. Studd, "being a commander in His Army, and not a chocolate soldier!" If we dare to name Him King, then we have to give Him permission to be the King that He is—every day of our lives. Then and only then will He produce His excellent likeness in us. So we are called to this excellence because He is excellent. "Be ye therefore perfect, even as your Father which is in heaven is perfect," said Jesus in Matthew 5:48.

The King Is Trustful

The King of Hearts in the Book of Proverbs trusted his queen. So would our King of Hearts in heaven trust us! This is what really blows my mind. God trusts us! Yes,

He does. He trusts us to come through for Him. He looks to us. Think about it for a minute. He trusts us with the Holy Spirit. He has not only sent His Spirit into our hearts crying, "Abba, Father," He has sent Him knowing our hearts are unholy. He trusts us then to be obedient to His holy promptings and hate the sin He hates, and repent of the selfishness He abhors. He trusts us to clean our spiritual house, just as diligently as the Proverbs woman cleaned her physical house.

Just as Jesus Christ took a whip and cleansed the temple in days long ago, He expects us to give Him permission to cleanse the temple that is His holy palace now—our bodies and our minds. We must let Him drive the money changers out, and the animals that have no business in the Lord's sweet house. All that goes on in the temple of our bodies which is not pleasing to the King must be cast out —overturned—redressed. Now He trusts us to give Him free rein to do that.

Not only does our King of Hearts trust us with His Spirit, He trusts us with His Son! "Christ in you," Paul says in wonder, "the hope of glory" (Colossians 1:27). What does this mean? It means Christ comes to live within our hearts when we invite Him to. It means the second Person of the Trinity is present with us. It means that we, like Mary, can say, "Behold the handmaiden of the Lord," and nurture as she did the new life of Christ within till "He be fully formed in us" (*see* Galatians 4:19). He trusts us to bid Him welcome, make Him feel at home, and settle Him down. Paul prayed the strangest prayer one day. He prayed for some new converts that "Christ may dwell in your hearts by faith . . ." (Ephesians 3:17). Was not Christ already dwelling in their hearts? Surely, but the secret lies in the word that the apostle used—the word *dwell*. The meaning is clear in the original language. It means to "settle down and feel at home."

He also trusts us to trust Him. Trust Him to keep our

kids safe on their dates; trust Him as we face major sur-
gery; trust Him to bring good out of evil. Once I realized
there was something I could do for God that would thrill
His heart I was, oh, so glad. After all, He had done so much
for me. And when you think about it, He doesn't ask much
of most of us—just childlike trust and dependence on
Him. The King of Hearts looks for that from his Queen.

The King Is Loving

Love cannot keep quiet. It has to tell of its love! The
King of Hearts in Proverbs 31 praised his wife. He loved
his Queen so thoroughly, he delighted to tell her so.

The King of heaven loves His Queen like that too. He
does not love blindly, for love is never blind. The heavenly King of Hearts knew the hands of men would nail
Him to a cross, but He also knew God would raise Him
from the dead and give Him back to those very same
hands. One day the centurion's hands, though stained
with the blood of God would be found clasped in prayer,
and the King would be satisfied. Love loves on—and on
—and on, knowing that "love never fails" (*see* 1 Corinthians 13:8) and He delights to tell us so.

Our heavenly King of Hearts is tender and sweet and
precious. He knows how to make us feel like a million
dollars when people tell us we're not worth a penny. He's
written us a very long and beautiful love letter. It's called
the Bible. What's more, we don't have to earn anything
for His favor. We don't have to charm Him, or pretend we
are something we're not, so He will like us. We don't have
to compete with other women for His attention, either.
All we have to do is be still and know that He is God. Just
be still enough—long enough—to be loved by His everlasting love. The love of God is shed abroad in a Queen
of Hearts' heart by the Holy Spirit, which is given unto us.
"I love you; I love you; I love you," the Spirit of the King

whispers—and this when others are shouting, *"I hate* you! I *hate* you! I *hate* you!"

The King Is Wise

The earthly King and Queen of Hearts in Proverbs knew very well that "the fear of the Lord is the beginning of knowledge" (Proverbs 1:7). The King of Hearts in heaven promises an ongoing revelation of wisdom because He *is* wisdom, and is a giving God. "Christ . . . is made unto us wisdom . . ." (1 Corinthians 1:30), Paul tells us. That ongoing revelation will never stop. What's more, He promises that what we know of Him down here is only the beginning. "Eye hath not seen, nor ear heard, neither have entered into the heart of man, the things which God hath prepared for them that love him," He promises in 1 Corinthians 2:9. That's why eternity will be so necessary. That's how long it's going to take to know all there is to know about our wise and wonderful heavenly King of Hearts. "The fear of the Lord is clean, enduring for ever . . ." sings the psalmist in 19:9. Yes, wisdom lasts forever.

The King Is Our Reward

So He is excellent, trustful, loving, and wise. He is also our Bridegroom, and the wedding day is coming!

The earthly King of Hearts is "known in the gates where he sits among the elders of the land." I cannot help but think of heaven when I read this verse. Our heavenly King of Hearts sits among the elders of His land, too. Remember, He is at home in heaven sitting upon His throne. But it was not always so. For thirty-three years that throne in heaven was empty, as He visited our earth to find His Bride—His Queen. He searched for her among the ladies of a land called "earth," until at last He found her! Her bride price was far above rubies, though the color was the same as the precious gem. The bride price was the precious blood He had to shed before He captured her heart.

Once found and won and paid for by His death upon the cross, the King of this earth ascended into heaven—a resurrected Husband. There He prepares a place for His beloved Bride. He's gone ahead to get the mansion ready! That's what He said. "In my Father's house are many mansions: if it were not so, I would have told you. I go to prepare a place for you. And if I go and prepare a place for you, I will come again, and receive you unto myself; that where I am, there ye may be also" (John 14:2,3). His Bride, the Church on earth has fine clothes of linen and scarlet just like the Proverbs 31 woman. The linen speaks of righteousness, the scarlet of the bride price.

Working and Watching

Just as the Queen of Hearts is depicted in Proverbs 31, happily and busily productive, so we must be as we wait for our King to come home at the end of our day! We must be out and about doing what would honor him the most. We may be tired, rising while it is yet night, our lamps going not out, because we know there is but little time left, but we will be watching for his appearing. There is such a little time to be the mother and wife we must be; the helper to the poor and forlorn; the skilled businesswoman. A sense of urgency and expectancy must pervade our earthly hearts as we redeem the time, for the days are evil. We, His earthly Queens must "occupy till He come" (see Luke 19:13), and remember that our heavenly King promises not to keep us waiting long. The Bride of Christ has no idea exactly what time her Lord will come to receive her to Himself and carry her away on angels' wings, that she might be forever at His side, but she is on tiptoe with her face toward the door.

Whatever time of the day or night her King may come, He must find her excelling. He must be able to trust her to love and to be wise, and He will undoubtedly love her and thank her for that. Then every Queen of Hearts on earth will earn her final great reward. The King of Hearts will meet her at the entrance to the celestial city gates. "Give her of the fruit of her hands; and let her own works praise her in the gates" (Proverbs 31:30), He will say. The fruit of her hand will be Jesus Christ. *He* Himself will be her exceeding great reward. She will not be with Him at the celestial city gates and among the elders of the heavenly land because of her works, but because the bride price was paid, and she has been married by faith to her heavenly Bridegroom.

Queen of hearts—
> **Lift up your head, your redemption draweth nigh—**
> **Behold your Bridegroom cometh!**

EVEN SO, COME, LORD JESUS—
KING OF OUR HEARTS!

WORKSHEET

Read these points to ponder from chapter 7 and spend five minutes doing so.

- Fearing God means we rightly fear His holiness, as we see we have come far short of the high standards He has set for us.

- We have a reverential awe for self that manifests itself in pride in all its forms because we are "of our father, the devil."

- We can even be religious and be of our father the devil.

- Satan knows that the ultimate satisfaction of the human heart is to hear God's "well done," and so he sets about us with subtle savagery, hoping for a "half-done," an "underdone," or an "undone" instead. He plays on our pride.

- What you do because you love and fear the Lord will bring respect if not praise.

- There is nothing that makes you feel quite so loved, warm, and complete as when God says, "Thank you."

- He trusts us to clean our spiritual house just as diligently as the Proverbs woman cleaned her physical house.

- God trusts us to trust Him.

- *"I love you; I love you; I love you,"* the Spirit of the King whispers and this when others are shouting, "I *hate* you! I *hate* you! I *hate* you!"

- Just as the Queen of Hearts is depicted in Proverbs 31 happily and busily productive, so we must be as we wait for our King to come home at the end of our day.

1. **Definition**
   Define the "fear of the Lord."

2. **Discussion**
   Read Luke 18:9–14 and discuss. Bring the story up to date.

3. **Diversion**
   How does Satan use praise to distract us from seeking to please God?

4. **Learning From Luke**
   Read Luke 1:34–45.
   a) What can you learn about fearing the Lord from Mary and Elizabeth?
   b) What can you learn about God?

5. **Divine Thanks**
   When has God said thank you to you? Share if appropriate.

6. **Divine Description**
   Describe the King of heaven. Which aspect of His character brings you most joy, and why?

7. **Praise and Prayer Time**

Praise, my soul, the King of heaven,
To His feet thy tribute bring;
Ransomed, healed, restored, forgiven,
Evermore His praises sing, Alleluia!
Alleluia! Praise the everlasting King!

HENRY F. LYTE